AIZER K'NEGDO

The Jewish Woman's Guide To Happiness In
Marriage

AIZER K'NEGDO

THE JEWISH WOMAN'S GUIDE TO HAPPINESS IN MARRIAGE

BY SARAH CHANA RADCLIFFE

Targum / Feldheim

First published 1988
ISBN 0-944070-08-6

Phototypeset at Targum Press

Published by:
Targum Press Inc.
22700 W. Eleven Mile Rd.
Southfield, Mich. 48034

Distributed by:
Philipp Feldheim Inc.
200 Airport Executive Park
Spring Valley, N.Y. 10977

Distributed in Israel by:
Nof Books Ltd.
POB 23646
Jerusalem 91235

Printed in Israel

Moshe Mordechai Lowy
Rabbi
Congregation Agudath Israel

בס״ד

משה מרדכי לאווי
מרא דאתרא
דק״ק אגודת ישראל טאראנטא

עש״ק פ' "לא טוב היות האדם לבדו אעשה לו עזר כנגדו„ ה'תשמ״ט פה
טאראנטא יצ״ו

    I have read and learned Mrs. Radcliffe's inspiring book [ספר]
"Aizer K'negdo" and found it to be a most helpful aizer in every sense
of the word. It will definitely be beneficial for חתנים and כלות who
are starting out and also very helpful for prolonging and enhancing
existing marriages. The book contains a wealth of information taken
from Torah sources (from חומש to the latest אחרונים), addressing every
issue pertinent to sustaining a beautiful Torah home. The realistic
examples with profound solutions and advice, will solve many a problem
and cause many a chuckle. I recommend that this book should be in every
Jewish home. It should be read before marriage and studied periodically
throughout the marriage.

    הבאת שלום, bringing peace and sustaining שלום between husband and
wife, is a מצוה of which the רבש״ע says, "Let my Name be defaced and
erased, in order to bring peace between man and his wife." Mrs.
Radcliffe has become a partner in this salient task and should be
commended. May she be זוכה to פירות בעוה״ז with the קרן קימת לעולם
הבא, as we say every day in ברכת התורה,
"אלו דברים שאדם אוכל פרותיהם בעולם חזה והקרן קימת לו לעוה״ב
וכו' והבאת שלום בין אדם לחברו ובן איש לאשתו„

בברכת התורה

אלה מרדכי לאווי

Beth Avraham Yoseph of Toronto

A FAMILY SYNAGOGUE EMPHASIZING
THE WARMTH OF TORAH TRADITION

CONGREGATION

BAYT

RABBI BARUCH TAUB

ב"ה

7 Cheshvan, 5749
October 18, 1988

The creation of Adam and Chava and the challenges of
Shalom Bayis between husband and wife are introduced
simultaneously at the very beginning of the Torah.
This is most instructive.   If the family is the
milieu for the fulfillment of Torah life then the
health of the Torah family is essential.   A
healthful marriage is attainable if there is a
clear understanding of respective roles and a sensitive
system of communication between two individuals
who care for each other.

Sara Chana Radcliffe has guided many couples to
develop a meaningful marriage relationship.   As
a family therapist meticulously adherent to Halacha,
she is properly qualified to present to the community
this timely "handbook" for marital happiness.

It is hoped that many will take advantage of this
creative guide thereby increasing the measure of
Shalom Bayis in our world.

RABBI BARUCH TAUB

613 Clark Avenue West, Thornhill, Ontario L4J 5V3 Telephone (416) 886-3810
Affiliated with The Union of Orthodox Jewish Congregations of America.
JOSEPH TANENBAUM SYNAGOGUE CENTRE

בית ספר תיכון „בית יעקב"

וסמינר למורות ע"ש ר' יעקב פרלמן ע"ה

BETH JACOB HIGH SCHOOL & JACOB PERLMAN TEACHERS SEMINARY

410 LAWRENCE AVENUE WEST · TORONTO, ONTARIO M5M 1C2 · TELEPHONE 787-4949

RABBI A. STEFANSKY, Principal

RABBI E. BRAUNER, Executive Director   בס"ד

RABBI M.J. BOBROWSKY, Immediate Past President

MOSHE NUSSBAUM, Co-President
ERNEST WERNER, Co-President
MOSHE REICHMANN, Vice President
MOSHE ZOLTY, Treasurer
D. d'ANCONA, Chairman of Education Committee
S. GELLIS, Secretary
I. ZLOTNICK, Special Functions

MEMBERS OF THE BOARD

M. Alon
I. Alter
C. Anisfeld
S. Anisfeld
Prof. E. Birnbaum
A. Bleeman
D. Drena
N. Elzas
B. Feintuch
M.F. Finkelstein
D. Friedberg
A. Gestetner
A. Grubner
Dr. A. Heber
D. Hendler
D. Hofstedter
G. Hofstedter
S. Hofstedter
D. Kleiner
Dr. T. Kohn
J. Kosoy
J. Kranz
G. Kuhl
H. Landau
J. Lebovics
Y.Y. Lev
M. Maierovits
H. Mandelbaum
H. Marder
J. Markovic
Mordche Nussbaum
M. Perlman
A. Rappaport
E. Reichman
A. Reichmann
E. Reichmann
R. Reichmann
S. Reichmann
A. Rosenblum
K. Rubner
W. Szydlow
H. Tennenbaum
Z. Tress
Rabbi S.K. Weinberg
I. Weinstock
S. Yunger
D. Zimmerman
B. Zolty

I am pleased that Mrs. Radcliffe has written a practical guide to Sholom Bayis. Her erudition and depth of perception qualify her emminently for this noble endeavor. Today's young husband and wife urgently need guidance in understanding each other's feelings, actions and reactions. Too many couples are deprived of marital bliss only because they are ignorant of some of the basic duties toward each other, nor are they aware of the profound pain they inflict upon the individual they love the most through their thoughtless actions.

I hope that this book will help the husband develop love and admiration for his wife and increase her happiness whenever possible as our Sages instruct. From Mrs. Radcliffe's words, may the wife learn to honor her husband, to keep anything displeasing out of his way and, as the Rambam says, to treat him as one treats royalty. This will undoubtedly lead to a harmonious life where children can grow in joy and happiness to an adulthood destined for greatness.

This text would be of immeasurable value for the Kallah and her instructor during the period of preparation for marriage.

Rabbi A. Stefansky,

Principal

Acknowledgments

I am deeply grateful to all of those who provided encouragement and assistance in the production of this book: to my husband, Avraham, for all of his technical assistance in the word-processing department and for his love and support; to my children for their co-operation and patience when I was busy writing; to Rav Yaakov Rapoport for his enthusiasm and direction; to Rabbi Shlomo Noach Mandel for his advice and help; to Aharon and Nechama Yachad; to Minna Sapirman, Nechama Silver, and Miriam Sweet-Goldstein, who provided inspiration and sound advice; to Rabbi Baruch Taub, Rabbi Akiva Stephansky and Rabbi Moshe Lowy for taking the time to review the manuscript; to Rabbi Moshe Silver and all of those who checked the footnotes of the text.

I would particularly like to thank Rabbi Yaakov Hirschman, Rosh Kollel of Toronto, who checked the manuscript for hashkofic and halachic accuracy and offered many valuable suggestions.

Sara Chana Radcliffe
Kislev, 5749

CONTENTS

CHAPTER ONE
Being an *Aizer K'negdo*

In describing the structure of marriage, the Torah tells us that woman was created to be an *aizer k'negdo*—a helpmate for her husband.[1] This being so, many questions present themselves. What kind of "help" is a woman supposed to provide for her spouse? If it is her job to "help," then what can she expect for herself in terms of marital happiness? Is she only to give and not to receive? What are her husband's obligations to her?

In fact, the notion that woman was created to help man and to be a companion for him sometimes leads people to imagine that the Torah views women simply as servants to their husbands—cooking and cleaning for them, fulfilling their every wish. Although many women do, in fact, make home-making their main occupation, it is not only this kind of assistance that makes a wife an *aizer k'negdo*. Rather, it is the unique strengths and spiritual characteristics of a woman which provide the "help" that a man requires and contribute to the formation of a happy marriage. The Torah tells us that man was incomplete before the creation of the *aizer k'negdo*; it does not say that woman was incomplete and in need of man. Thus, JUST BY BEING HERSELF, as *Hashem* created her, a woman can be of help to her husband. This helping function enhances the marital relationship as we shall soon see. However, it does not create a one-way situation in which the wife helps the husband while he does nothing for her. Although she may not need the help of her husband in the same way, a wife obviously does need his love and support. The Torah commands him to give her this. A Jewish husband is obligated to treat his wife with the utmost respect and kindness. She, too, is to treat her husband lovingly. When husband and wife fulfill their mutual obligations to each other, they create *shalom bayis*—a happy and peaceful home.

Yet, beyond this reciprocal love relationship, a woman's "help" plays a specific role in the creation and maintenance of marital harmony. To understand the impact of a woman's help upon her marriage, we must examine more closely the nature of the assistance that she provides. The Torah illustrates the helping power of women in many instances. It was Sarah who made the important decision to separate her son Yitzchak from Avraham's other child Yishmael.[2] She, not Avraham, possessed understanding of the potentially harmful effects of the influence of one child upon the other. It was the child Miriam who encouraged her parents to continue to have children despite Pharaoh's evil decrees.[3] Her own father did not share her depth of perception, but relied on her insight and followed her advice. It was the women of the desert generation, not the men, who refused to participate in the sin of the golden calf.[4] The son of Peles was saved from the disaster that befell Korach only because his wife wisely advised him to remove himself from the fatal dispute.[5] These are just a few of the many times that we see how the special intuition and understanding of women provided assistance to their men. This, then, is the "help" that woman provides, a by-product of woman's very nature.

Within marriage, a woman's natural intuition, understanding, and disposition function to help her husband and to enhance her marital relationship. In order to see how this is so, let us look at the nature of Jewish marriage and the responsibilities of husband and wife within that sacred union. Everything that goes on inside the home has the potential to radiate Torah. The decoration of the house, the activities that occur there, and every mundane conversation can reflect Torah ideals. The love and kindness which can characterize husband-wife interactions is the essence of Torah itself. It is in this area, therefore, that a wife may be of greatest assistance. A husband is obligated by the Torah to fulfill all the laws *bein adam l'chavero* (between man and his fellow) when interacting with his own wife. Yet it is she, whose natural sensitivity and insight make her an expert in the realm of interpersonal relationships, who can provide the help for her husband in this very domain!

This "help" increases marital happiness for both husband and wife since the Jewish marriage is ideally characterized by interdependency rather than independence. Rather than being an individual who happens to be living with another individual, a Jewish woman is part of her husband, intimately attached to him on the spiritual level. He and she are "one" in essence and purpose. Therefore, any help that a wife gives her husband really helps them both. Just as a woman who helps her husband by providing extra income also benefits her own life style, a woman who helps her husband spiritually benefits her own spiritual life as well. If she helps him to become a kinder, more considerate human being, then obviously she herself will benefit from his improvement.

Therefore, as an *aizer k'negdo*, a woman must try not to resent the fact that her husband does not always live up to her expectations and standards in his personal conduct. (She herself no doubt disappoints him on occasion as well!) Rather, she should endeavor to accept the challenge to help him come closer to Torah ideals and fulfill his spiritual potential. While she has neither the sole responsibility nor the complete power to make her marriage work, *Hashem* has provided her with special qualities which enable her to be a positive influence within the relationship. By simply being herself—but striving to be her BEST possible self—a woman can help her husband to become his best possible self. Even when people strive to be their best, they will still possess many human failings (for such is the nature of mankind), but the efforts they make toward *middos* improvement inevitably make them better people than they would otherwise be. This improvement cannot help but have a positive impact on marital contentment.

Striving to improve oneself is, of course, an enormous challenge. Women are not angels, but human beings who must struggle with their own weaknesses and faults. Moreover, a woman lives with another human being—a man with his own set of imperfections. She might be reluctant to give of herself to her husband if she is not confident that he will treat her in a loving fashion in return. She may defensively withhold her warmth and kindness from him, becoming a "helpmate OPPOSITE" him—against him rather than for him. This cycle is actually very natural. If a husband makes his wife unhappy, she is inclined to retaliate in kind. She instinctively responds in a way which says, "You're not nice to me, so I won't be nice to you." In this way, the couple makes each other miserable.

On the other hand, when a woman accepts the challenge of being an *aizer k'negdo* and continues to work on her own *middos* and elevate her own behavior (despite what she sees in her husband), she may find that her husband eventually changes his behavior pattern as well. He may begin to emulate her good example, or at least build up enough trust and positive feeling toward her that he will be able to alter his position. Moreover, her direct efforts in negotiating issues, explaining her needs and desires, and teaching her husband how to meet them, also increase the likelihood that her husband will be able to bring her happiness. Our Sages tell us that Dina would have been able to change the *rasha* Eisav into a good man had she married him, because a good woman influences her husband in a very positive way.[6] This is not to say that a husband should passively wait for his wife to show him the way—he should be working hard toward establishing *shalom bayis* at all times. Whether he does this or not, however, a wife should keep in mind that her own influence, both passive and active, may eventually be successful in facilitating change. Of course, a woman must also realize that it sometimes takes years to see the direct results of her "positive influence." Thus if she gives her husband only six months to "change his ways," the marriage may not survive to witness the change.

Fortunately, being an *aizer k'negdo* does not require that a woman be "super-human" and "super-tolerant." It only requires that she be herself. She needn't be a paradigm of human virtue—only a woman with normal strengths and weaknesses. For as a woman, she INHERENTLY possesses those traits which can be a positive influence on her husband. In fact, the *aizer k'negdo* is far from a passive, suffering person who endures all kinds of indignity and unhappiness for the sake of *shalom bayis*! Rather, the *aizer k'negdo* is a strong, purposeful woman who uses all of her talents and skills to be the best marriage partner she can be. She actively works to bring happiness into her own life and into her marriage. She implores *Hashem* to grant her efforts with success, knowing that the ultimate outcome is up to Him.

Does this imply, then, that happiness in marriage is totally dependent on the wife's performance? Not at all. We know from Torah sources, as well as from common sense, that husbands have at least an equal role in creating *shalom bayis*. Some opinions hold that a husband's obligations in this area are even greater than his wife's.[7] It takes the very hard work of two dedicated people to create a happy home. If, however, one partner is not working toward this goal at a particular point in time, it does not mean that happiness is forever unattainable. Certainly their marital satisfaction must be temporarily marred. It is possible, however, for the situation to improve.

This is not to say that women should, in the fashion of martyrs, patiently suffer an intolerable relationship without seeking relief. Since the attainment of *shalom bayis* is such a great mitzvah, a couple must do everything possible to achieve it, and great patience must be expended in working toward it. Outside help from rabbis and trusted counselors may sometimes be necessary. Despite the presence of marital conflict, however, a woman can still strive to fulfill her own Torah obligations, including the laws concerning relations between one's fellow and oneself. These laws pertain directly to her dealings with her husband. Even if he behaves in ways unacceptable to her and contrary to Torah guidelines, she is in no way exempt from behaving in accordance with halachah. His failure does not provide an excuse for her own failure. Moreover, her only chance for happiness in life is to refuse to fail. She must continue to be her best self for her own sake as well as for the sake of her marriage. If, in the end, it is *Hashem*'s will that she lacks the power to influence her husband positively, she has the comfort of knowing that she has not transgressed, that she has in fact done all that a wife can do, and that she has earned merit for her efforts.

For this reason, it is valid to write a book on marriage addressed to women only. Although everything contained in this book is equally applicable to men, it is addressed to you, the *aizer k'negdo*. You can take direct control of only your behavior—not your husband's. You can make changes in your own *middos*—not his. Moreover, it is futile to try and improve someone else; the most we can hope to do is influence another person to make changes in himself. Although you may have many ideas about how your husband could change for the better, you cannot implement them. You can only make yourself change for the better. As your communication style alters, however, the entire system of husband-wife communication alters as well. He must respond to a different set of words and behaviors. This necessitates a change on his part, one that contains within it the possibility for growth toward greater marital happiness. The job of the *aizer k'negdo* is to do her best in her own sphere, elevating her own *middos*, and establishing the correct atmosphere for a Torah home. With *Hashem*'s help, her efforts will be successful in facilitating the growth of true marital happiness.

What is Marital Happiness?

It is important to define the goal we are working toward. *Shalom bayis* is not only the absence of marital strife. In fact, no marriage is without moments of dissension. However, a truly unhappy marriage is CHARACTERIZED by discontentment and disharmony, manifested in everyday issues. In other words, simple conversation may be tense and unpleasant, while large unresolved issues cast a grey gloom over the atmosphere. There may be frequent disagreements or emotional outbursts. Both partners suffer pain and withdrawal from each other. Conflicts are handled in a destructive fashion; the hurtful negotiations destroy the fabric of the marriage.

On the other hand, marital harmony is characterized by a mood of general cooperation and satisfaction, warmth and trust. The husband and wife feel affection toward each other, enjoy each other's company, share a sense of purpose and direction, and feel free to live their lives fully. Their home environment is relaxed and pleasant; good humor and good will pervade the atmosphere.

Even the happiest of marriages is in constant flux, however, with many trying and challenging periods between the calmer and more pleasant moments. When these rough periods are negotiated smoothly, trust is enhanced and the marriage bonds are strengthened. Happy marriages are those in which conflicts are resolved without undue emotional pain. Differences of opinion do not threaten the union, but rather contribute to its multifaceted nature. Just as one person may experience many different thoughts and desires, a strong marriage can contain differing values and interests. Sameness is not a prerequisite for marital harmony. Only loving intentions and actions are necessary to channel the different energies into positive directions.

Thus, marital happiness is not a constant state of euphoria. It is a working relationship devoted to building marital love—a form of companionship, support system, and intimate relationship based on Torah goals. This love permits each partner to experience feelings of comfort, safety, and meaning while offering room for individual growth and expression. The marriage operates within a framework of general optimism and trust, which husband and wife utilize to help them cope with everyday challenges. A strong commitment to Torah, marriage, and family life characterizes the entire relationship, providing strength and direction. This commitment ensures that the couple will endeavor to work through each difficulty they encounter, trusting in *Hashem*'s help.

Naturally, divorce is not considered by such couples to be a possible solution to marital distress. Marriage is seen as a permanent relationship. Although the Torah does permit divorce as a *refuah* when all efforts at reconciliation have failed, it is certainly not a preferable outcome. When a couple struggle with all their might to overcome conflict and attain *shalom bayis*, they earn a great reward both in this world and in *olam ha'bah*. Indeed, there are almost no lasting unions which have not weathered rough periods. In successful relationships, the partners have worked through these times to reach an improved way of relating. Sometimes this process requires years of effort. Moreover, there are couples who only begin to enjoy marital happiness after they have shared many significant life events together, and this, too, takes time. Only when a deep commitment to marital permanence exists is it possible for husband and wife to allow themselves the time necessary to grow into *shalom bayis.*

How To Use This Book

Within a framework of commitment, you can begin to explore options in techniques of communication and behavior. This book presents both a philosophy of marriage and a series of practical marriage techniques. As you read each technique, ask yourself if this is something you want to experiment with. If it is a technique which you would like to work on, concentrate on that one new behavior for several days. Don't try several new techniques at once, but rather wait until you've made some progress with one at a time. It is best to make small improvements in a step-by-step, organized way, rather than attempt a big, overwhelming change which will be beyond your abilities. Always permit yourself to make mistakes. Some techniques involve no more than learning to reword a request, while others are close to changing an entire *middah.* With any change, progress is accompanied by regressions. Be encouraging and supportive of yourself. If you are unsuccessful at first, persevere and reward yourself for your perseverance. If you say something or do something your "old" way by mistake, you can always say, "Wait. I want to try that again. What I meant to say (do) was..."

Similarly, do not look for instantaneous new responses in your husband. His reaction to new behaviors on your part may range from surprise to outrage to apathy. Be patient with him also. If he reads this book (as he is welcome to do) his progress may be faster. Do not, however, insist that he read it. Particularly, do not show him the page on which his *aveiros* are located. Using the book like this will only undermine your goal of working toward greater *shalom bayis*. You can be sure that changes in him will occur at an even slower rate than your own changes, but do not get discouraged. It might be a good idea to start off by working on the *middah* of patience.

One hazard of any self-improvement plan is that a person may come to feel defeated at the outset. As you read over the suggested techniques in this book, it is possible you will feel that you are currently doing "everything" wrong and that you will not be able to improve in so many areas. Alternatively, you may feel that it is unreasonable to expect people to try to be so pleasant or so kind—that it is somehow demanding too much. Another common experience is to feel that normal human inadequacies (such as moodiness, short-temper, impatience, intolerance, and so on) render you inadequate as a wife or person and that nothing less than total perfection is acceptable. All of these attitudes are aided and abetted by the *yetzer hara*, which loves failure and defeat. Although these are natural reactions, we can only work on self-improvement if we begin by accepting and supporting ourselves as we are. A woman does not have to become a perfect person in order to attain marital happiness! (Her husband doesn't have to be a perfect person either!) It is not necessary for her to be constantly smiling, constantly giving in, constantly boosting her husband's ego. On the contrary, she must have the courage to ask for what she needs and the self-respect to remain authentic. There is room for her to be a natural person with moments of irritation, selfishness, and even depression. After all, what person does not experience these kinds of emotions? In marriage, it is only important that negative characteristics do not DOMINATE the relationship; rather, the relationship must be characterized by a positive atmosphere if happiness is to be achieved.

Self-improvement plans are only appropriate and desirable when you notice that there is room for improvement in a specific area—in other words, when you yourself are dissatisfied with the kinds of interactions which are occurring. Therefore every technique in this book will not necessarily be relevant to your specific situation. If things are going well, leave them alone! Continue to be yourself! Only when a particular point strikes home should you consider experimenting with changes in behavior. If you feel phony in your first attempts with a new technique, persevere. This is a normal reaction. However, if you continue to feel unnatural after several weeks, either modify or discontinue the technique. It's important to be yourself!

Techniques for Developing Marital Happiness

Happy relationships are the result of behaving and communicating in predominantly constructive ways. The Torah is the source of the required behaviors for successful social interactions; it outlines all of the permissible and desirable behaviors of human beings toward each other. The basis of all of these laws is kindliness. As Hillel phrased it: "Do not do unto others what you would not want them to do unto you."[8] Torah attitudes are as important as the behaviors themselves. Many proper attitudes are outlined in Rabbi Pliskin's book *Gateway to Happiness,*[9] a suitable companion text to this manual. With the combination of correct thinking and correct acting—in other words, by developing her own *middos*—a woman does all that is possible in working toward a successful marriage. She fulfills her potential as an *aizer k'negdo*, providing the best influence that she can. Her husband must do the rest!

In this book, the techniques of communication and behavior relevant to marital harmony are organized into four categories:

1. establishing respect
2. building trust
3. creating affection
4. developing intimacy

These categories contain within them the Torah language, strategies, and actions which provide the basis for successful marriage. All of them are learnable. With *Hashem*'s help, the use of these techniques will result in increased marital happiness for you and your husband.

Please note: The examples in this book show the wife behaving in both undesirable ways and desirable ways, while the husband's behavior is normally portrayed as neutral (with a few exceptions). This is not to imply that husbands don't behave in undesirable ways! Since the book is addressed to wives, it is the wife's behavior which is being examined. However, all of the examples could be read with the roles of husband and wife reversed. Any behavior which is recommended for the wife is equally recommended for the husband.

CHAPTER TWO
Establishing Respect

According to Torah thought, a Jewish woman should respect her husband. The Rambam writes that a woman should regard her husband as a king.[1] In fact, every woman wants to be able to look up to and admire her spouse. Yet as she lives in daily contact with a man, a woman sees much that she finds hard to respect. Perhaps he eats in an unpleasant manner or doesn't clean up after himself. Perhaps he appears lax in the observance of certain *mitzvos*. Maybe he lacks business ability or makes obvious errors in judgment. It may be that he continuously misplaces his glasses and his keys, is overly harsh in his discipline of the children, doesn't manage his time effectively, or displays a host of other major and minor human weaknesses. The wife sees not a "king," but simply a human being. Feelings of contempt may replace feelings of respect as a result of the intense familiarity between husband and wife.

On the other hand, it is not so difficult to respect a stranger. In fact, we usually manage to treat our friends, colleagues, distant relatives, and others with whom we come into superficial contact in a respectful manner. Since we don't know these people so well, we still respect them. Unfortunately, our closeness to our spouse results in a state of mutual relaxation which exposes all weaknesses. As a wife sees her husband's faults, she makes fewer efforts to hide her own. No longer an "eager-to-please" new bride, she becomes her "real self." Of course, a "real self" can be rather unpleasant at times. However, a husband still has a normal set of feelings even though he has been married for a while. It still matters to him how his wife speaks to him and what she says. If a woman wants to enjoy happiness in marriage, it is more important—not less important—for her to be careful of her husband's feelings than of anyone else's. Since she is generally able to control her speech and actions for the benefit of others, she must learn to use this same control for the benefit of the most important person in her life!

Why is respect so important? Actually, respect is the foundation upon which love rests. In itself, respect does not make for happiness in a marriage. However, without respect, true happiness cannot develop. Respect is the characteristic of a relationship which allows for the growth of positive feelings. Lack of respect stunts or prevents this growth. A woman who does not respect her husband cannot come to love him. Thus, it is essential that a wife cultivate the ability to respect her mate. However, if a woman does not currently respect her husband, what will enable her to change her attitude? Assuming he does not make any significant changes which render him more "respectable," is it possible for her to learn to respect him nonetheless?

There are, in fact, several strategies a wife can use to increase her ability to respect her husband just as he is. To begin with, she might think of specific behaviors (or techniques") that she can implement. Instead of thinking to herself, "I simply can't respect my husband" (for whatever reasons), let her think in terms of individual actions that she can perform. Each act of kindness to another person is considered a mitzvah—a form of chessed.[2] Each display of thoughtful and respectful behavior fulfills the mitzvah of "Love your fellow man as yourself."[3] Thus, she need only fulfill her Torah obligations in dealing with her husband. (The Torah teaches us to behave in a kind fashion to all human beings.) By acting respectfully toward her husband (rather than feeling respect for him), she will eventually come to feel respect as well. Although her respectful behavior techniques may not originally be motivated by a feeling of respect for her husband, they can lead to the very respect she lacks.

Secondly, a woman can consider the teaching of our Sages that her husband is her bashert chosen by Hashem Himself. This does not mean that Hashem has selected a perfect mate for one's satisfaction and enjoyment. Rather, one's husband is perfect in the sense of being the exact person required to help one reach one's spiritual perfection. Hashem knows which strengths and weaknesses in a husband will help to fulfill the wife's spiritual potential. For example, an impatient girl may grow into a patient woman through the experience of living with a certain kind of man. Many *middos* may be similarly elevated and refined through the challenge of living with one's spouse. Instead of looking at the faults and foibles of her husband and coming to disdain him because of them, a wife can attempt to see how this "fault" may play a role in helping her to improve herself. This orientation, too, can help a wife come to respect her spouse.

A third consideration is that respect is not an all-or-nothing proposition. A woman should not fall into the trap of thinking in condemning patterns such as, "I don't respect my husband." Certainly there may be some things that a wife doesn't respect about her mate, but there is no need to conclude that therefore there is nothing to respect about him! Suppose that he is a terribly rude person who does not speak to his wife in a proper, refined fashion. Even then his wife can find things to respect in him. Although his communication skills need obvious improvement, it may be that he is a hard worker, a devoted father, and a generous host. He may have many redeeming and respectful characteristics. Since every person has faults, no marriage could endure if each spouse concluded that faults render their mate totally unacceptable. A healthier strategy for a wife to pursue is to think to herself, "I don't respect this or that quality in my husband. However, I do respect these and those."

The final consideration is the most important of all. A WOMAN MUST RESPECT HER HUSBAND'S LIMITATIONS. This is the crucial element of respect. Basically, it means that a wife understands and accepts who her husband is and what his role is in her life. She also understands what a husband is not. If a woman expects her husband to be her best friend, her psychologist, and her mentor, and finds that he is none of these things to her, then her disappointment will be keen. She will feel that he has let her down, and she will disrespect him for not being able to fulfill her needs adequately. Thus, unrealistic expectations may lead a wife to disrespect her husband. What, then, can a woman reasonably expect of a husband?

To answer this question, let us examine the nature of a typical man and compare it to the nature of a typical woman. Then we will analyze the role of each sex within Jewish marriage and, in so doing, will come to understand both the assets and the limitations of a husband. Since we are speaking in generalities, we must acknowledge at the outset that there will be many exceptions to what we are about to say. Nonetheless, some general trends can be described.

Men tend to be logical, steady creatures. They are not known for exceptional sensitivity to the moods and needs of others, but this very trait often leads them to a position of easy-going acceptance of those around them. They will, for example, be patient and accepting of a spouse, overlooking many flaws. They tend also to be optimists as far as their marital relationship goes, expecting that many difficulties can be overlooked and overcome (perhaps because they do not perceive so many levels and depths of conflicts and emotions). Men are good at doing one thing at a time with intense concentration[4] and have the ability to devote their energies to very demanding projects and endeavors. Although possessing muscular strength, men tend to be vulnerable physically, succumbing to more syndromes and illnesses than women and suffering more intensely from their ailments.

Women are actually very different from men. They function in an intensely emotional mode, being highly sensitive to social cues and interpersonal relationships of all kinds. They tend to be more critical and less accepting than men and therefore less optimistic in their marital spheres. Women are capable of doing many things at one time, to divide their attention and energies into several directions simultaneously.[5] Although lacking muscular strength, women have good physical endurance and are able to sustain higher levels of pain and discomfort.

Obviously *Hashem* created men and women differently in order for them to be able to fulfill their unique tasks in life. A woman is well suited to the demands of household management, which require the ability to handle many competing demands and require skills in many different areas, as well as the nurturing of her family members, which requires astute interpersonal awareness. A man is suited to pursue specific goals requiring steady, dependable energy in a focused task. Together they can create a unit devoted to building a Jewish household. In marriage, a husband and wife become as one, as *Hashem* commanded: "And they shall be one flesh." They need each other in order to be able to achieve their separate and mutual spiritual goals. Husband and wife have an interdependent relationship which offers benefits to each. When a woman understands the nature of the benefits she can expect her husband to bring, she will have a much clearer perception of his limitations as well.

What, then, are these benefits? A man has many well-established benefits from the marriage union. His wife "gives light to his eyes and stands him on his feet."[6] In other words, by running the household efficiently she permits him a free and uncluttered mind, enabling him to function effectively in his sphere. "An attractive home, an attractive wife, and attractive vessels open up a man's mind."[7] He can concentrate on his endeavors. A wife's encouragement and emotional support can help a man reach his potential.[8] That she takes care of his young children is so important that the Talmud tells us Rabbi Chiya considered it a sufficient characteristic of a wife even if she lacked any other positive attributes![9]

In fact, a woman also benefits enormously from the marriage union. Indeed, she needs to be clearly aware of the way in which she benefits if she is to be able to appreciate and respect her partner. Unfortunately, a woman sometimes fails to perceive the benefits her husband brings her because of the inconsistency between the fantasy she had of marriage before she became a wife and the reality as she now experiences it.

To begin with, a young, unmarried woman may expect that her future husband will think, feel, and function like she does. She has had female friends all her life who have been strong sources of support and affection. She imagines that a husband will be like a special woman friend—in fact, her best friend. She anticipates that he will share her perceptions and understand her emotions.

Imagine her disappointment if she discovers that her husband's interests are very different from hers, that he doesn't understand her feelings and concerns, that he doesn't solve problems the way she does, that he doesn't reach the same conclusions that she does. She may find that she disagrees with his opinions and differs in her assessment of priorities. Since she is comfortable with her own perceptions, she feels that he is wrong (rather than different) on many occasions. His position in the community may not be what she thinks it should be; he may not be the man she imagined he would be. She develops a feeling of superiority, which, combined with her domestic responsibilities, leaves her feeling that she is, in fact, taking care of her husband. Many women with children actually feel that their husband is like another child in the family! Thus, a woman's innate nurturing abilities lead her to feel like a mother, even to her own husband. This results in lack of respect. A woman must be able to accept her nurturing functions without losing respect for the recipient of her care— but how?

One way is for her to consciously focus on the "good" that a husband brings to his wife, the benefits she receives from him. If women accept what men have to offer, they actually find much to respect and appreciate. There are many basics that a husband provides simply by taking on the role of husband. Although a woman is a highly competent creature, well able to set up her own home environment and maintain herself in business, she feels incomplete without a husband. It is in her nature to desire to make a home with a man. Even a man's simple presence in the house can offer the comfort of human companionship. Moreover, she requires a husband in order to be able to have children. She wants to fulfill her biological potential and has a craving to nurture offspring and pass on to them their rich heritage; she intensely desires a husband with whom to make these ambitions come to life. Indeed, a Torah life style is best lived in partnership, with each partner fulfilling his or her specific *mitzvos*.

The list of benefits of a husband includes many other practical and functional considerations as well: he provides some measure of physical protection from outside dangers, for which a wife is grateful; a husband who supports a wife financially permits her to be a *balabusta* and to derive great satisfaction from that role; men often handle tough discipline problems in a superior fashion, due to their patience, cool, and logic (as well as the fact that they haven't been home all day!); they sometimes have useful talents and skills (home repair, auto mechanics, bookkeeping) and may provide assistance in the way of shopping, driving, food preparation, and child care. This is all apart from whatever companionship and friendship they offer and special attributes and traits which they possess. If a woman looks at what her husband has to offer, rather than what he lacks, she can be very satisfied and pleased. In fact, "the only way to have a happy life is to keep your eyes focused on what you have and not on what you are lacking."[10] Thus a woman should refrain from thinking in terms of her husband's failures and weaknesses, and develop a gratitude and respect for the functions he does perform in her life.

Having established this respect, however, a woman may nonetheless feel that her husband does not meet all of her needs. This is only natural, since no one person can fulfill all the needs of another and because men were not created with a developed set of nurturing abilities. In fact, men are, in general, ill-suited to fulfill many female needs.

There are two main ways in which women can meet extra needs for nurturing and like-minded stimulation. One thing a woman can do is establish a close friendship with another woman! Women enjoy talking about issues, conflicts, and challenges. Women understand each other, and are good at nurturing each other. A woman can discuss anything with a female friend (except her relationship with her husband—this should be kept private, made known only to a mutually agreed upon Rav or counselor). A wife will not love her husband less because of the support she receives from a friend. On the contrary, she may love and respect him more because she values him for what he does give her and she accepts and respects his limitations. She doesn't bother him with what doesn't interest him. She doesn't frustrate him by asking him to be something that he is not. She doesn't anger herself by blaming him for being what he is.

A second strategy that a woman can use effectively is to teach her husband how to communicate with her in the way that she wants. Instead of hoping that he will one day understand and deliver what she wants, she TELLS him specifically how to meet her needs. She may say she needs time, eye contact, verbal feedback, approval, sympathy, or encouragement. She can ask for whatever she likes, and she can teach him how to give it. Many men improve their interpersonal skills as a result of living with a good "teacher." Of course, a good teacher is patient! These techniques will be elaborated upon in the "Techniques" section of this manual. The thing to understand at this point is that a healthy respect for a husband's limitations leads to a greater respect for him as a husband.

Let us now begin to examine specific respect-building techniques and their application in marriage. These techniques fall into two broad categories: those which are general and pertain to all occasions, and those which have special relevance to times of disagreement or dispute. We will begin with the former category.

Techniques

1. Acknowledge Your Husband's Presence

This is a fairly simple technique to begin with, but one which demonstrates basic respect. Women are busy people. Whether they work outside the home or within it, women are seldom idle. They may be busy with young children, occupied on the phone with community work, cooking, cleaning, mending, studying, working, shopping, banking, corresponding, or whatever—but they are seldom doing just nothing at all. Thus, when a husband telephones or enters the home, he can expect to find his wife occupied. Oddly enough, he may continue to be surprised by this fact for many years. He has arrived, so he expects and desires her attention.

Although she is indeed busy, it is totally disrespectful for her to ignore his presence. Ignoring involves any action which does not actively acknowledge his arrival and make him feel welcomed. If anyone else came to the door, she would certainly put down her broom, phone, or papers for a moment and speak with him however briefly. This is the respect one gives a stranger. A wife must endeavor to give her husband this same sort of acknowledgment.

Another challenge for a woman is to be able to acknowledge her husband's need for attention when there are little children around. Children's high-pitched whining seems to demand immediate response, but in actuality there are few emergencies which require prompt attention. The children can be told to wait a moment while Mother speaks to Father. A few carefully chosen words to your husband can then let him know that you are aware of his presence and his needs and will be able to attend to them shortly.

The issue of attention can also arise when two active people attempt to pursue their own interests. For example, a wife may have an intense desire to read (or her husband might). If one person reads at the breakfast table, interpersonal communication is naturally going to be stifled. Thus, a wife who reads while her husband sits beside her is paying more attention to her book than to her spouse. She may be losing a valuable opportunity to build closeness with him; moreover, he may feel that his presence is unimportant to her. Apart from weakening bonds of affection, ignoring one's partner in this way conveys basic disrespect. However, this is not to say that whenever husband and wife are together in the same room they need to be interacting with each other. Rather, it refers only to when they are involved in the same activity together (e.g., eating). At such times they should endeavor to share the activity. At times when they are obviously pursuing individual activities (e.g., one is writing letters and the other is reading), they can acknowledge each other's presence simply by smiling occasionally or making a remark once in a while. After all, marriage should ideally permit each spouse to fulfill individual potential through the active pursuit of interests, skills, and talents. A wife should simply remember to give her husband the acknowledgment he deserves even while she is in the midst of her active life.

Here are some examples of the right and wrong ways to handle the issue of acknowledging one's husband:

Example 1

wrong:

> husband: *"Hi! I'm home!"*

> wife: *"I'm busy with Shmuley."*

right:

> husband: *"Hi! I'm home!"*

> wife: *"Oh, hi Avi! I'll be downstairs in a second; I'm just taking care of Shmuley in the bathroom. I'll be right with you!"*

Example 2

wrong:

> *husband: "Leah, let's discuss our Chol HaMoed outing."*
>
> *wife: "Shoshy, stop licking your plate, please."*
>
> *husband: "Did you have any places in mind?"*
>
> *wife: "What? Asher, please eat your potatoes. Sit down, Levi."*
>
> *husband: "I said, did you have any places in mind?"*
>
> *wife: "Places in mind for what?"*

right:

> *husband: "Leah, let's discuss our Chol HaMoed outing."*
>
> *wife: "That sounds great Avi. Let me finish giving the kids dinner and I'll meet you in the den in about fifteen minutes, O.K.?"*

Comment:

The wife can make her husband feel acknowledged just by answering his first comment directly and, if necessary, letting him know that she can't continue a conversation at that specific moment. Telling him when she will be available lets him know that she is interested in what he has to say. Responding to him rather than ignoring him makes him feel respected.

2. Support Your Spouse in Public Situations

Great disrespect is shown when a person corrects his or her spouse in public. For the purpose of our discussion, "public" includes the presence of anyone other than the couple themselves and refers equally to strangers and to the children of the couple. Thus, if a husband makes a statement with which the wife disagrees, it is disrespectful for her to announce her disagreement in front of other people, including her own children. In fact, the "rightness" of any parental statement or action is almost always of less significance to the children's psychological well-being than the opportunity to witness respect between their parents. Corrections and differences of opinion should always be discussed in private, later.

The main reason for being careful about this is that lack of support, or active contradiction, may cause one's husband embarrassment. The Torah forbids us to embarrass anyone.[11] Although we are forbidden to embarrass someone even in private,[12] public embarrassment is such a great offence that it is punishable by the loss of *olam ha'bah.*[13] These laws pertain to embarrassing anyone at all, but we also learn that one must be especially careful not to cause embarrassment to one's spouse.[14]

Example 1

wrong:

> *husband (in the presence of some neighbors): "Our daughter really enjoys school this year."*
>
> *wife: "No she doesn't. She's always complaining."*

right:

> *husband: "Our daughter really enjoys school this year."*
>
> *wife: "And how does your little girl like school, Mr. Gold?"*

Example 2

wrong:

> *husband (in a group situation): "Cheese is a terrific food to buy for the kids because it's so inexpensive."*

wife: "You can see he never does the shopping. Cheese is very expensive!"

right:

husband: "Cheese is a terrific food to buy for the kids because it's so inexpensive."

wife: "What do you fill your gang up with?"

Comment:

In the school episode the wife disagrees with her husband's opinion, but doesn't say anything about it in the "right" example. Later that day, she may ask him why he thinks their daughter likes school while she notices that she complains so much. Alternatively, she may decide that the issue isn't worth mentioning. In fact, most things are not worth making a fuss about, and remembering this can help one refrain from making corrections at all.

Occasionally, a woman feels that she just must correct her husband's statement since it is so blatantly wrong. He may announce, for example, that cheese is a good food to buy for the kids because it is so cheap. Since she does the shopping, she realizes that cheese is actually a very expensive commodity. If she says to those present that cheese is not actually cheap at all, she will have the satisfaction of being right. However, she can attain this satisfaction only if she is willing to disrespect and possibly embarrass her husband. She can really attain much greater satisfaction if she learns to monitor her speech and avoid *aveiros*, being careful to support her husband when in public with him.

3. Be on Time

It is very disrespectful to keep people waiting. In fact, it is considered one of the aspects of the mitzvah of "Love your fellow man"[15] not to keep people waiting.[16] When a wife is not on time, her husband is inconvenienced. Inconveniencing one's mate shows lack of consideration, which eventually is experienced as a sort of lack of love, since we don't hurt people we care about. If you are in the careless habit of detaining your partner, work on yourself to be five or ten minutes early for each mutual engagement you have. For example, if your husband says he will be home at 6:00 p.m. for dinner, make sure that you are ready for him at 5:50. If you and he are supposed to leave the house to attend a function at 5:45, make sure you are ready at 5:35. If you arrange to pick him up at the bus stop at 7:30, be there at 7:20. When you consistently aim to be ten minutes early for all of your appointments, you will soon find that you are on time for everything!

Some people are late, not as a careless oversight, but as a life style. Such people have always been late for everything ever since they were children. Despite efforts in adulthood, including professional help, they have never been successful in changing this pattern. If this describes you, you can still show consideration and respect for your husband. Your lateness need not inconvenience him. Make separate arrangements to go places and return from places. Don't make any mutual plans for anything. The two of you can run your lives on separate schedules if necessary. Although this sounds awkward and unnatural, it is certainly preferable to having recurrent arguments and confrontations regarding missed appointments and delays.

Example 1

wrong:

> husband: "I've been waiting for you for twenty minutes already!"

> wife: "I was ready fifteen minutes ago, but then you started studying your Gemara so I decided to wash a few more dishes. I've been waiting for you for ten minutes now!"

right:

> husband: "It's important to me to be on time for the wedding tonight. If you're ready to leave by 7:30, let's go together in the car. But if you're not ready by then, I'll call a taxi and you can meet me there later, O.K.?"

> wife: "That sounds reasonable. I'll try to be ready before 7:30 so I can go with you."

Example 2

wrong:

> husband: "You were almost half an hour late! I was really getting worried already!"

> wife: "Oh, I was caught up in traffic. You shouldn't have worried."

right:

> husband: "You were almost half an hour late! I was really getting worried already!"

> wife: "I'm really sorry I worried you. I guess I should have left earlier. I didn't allow enough time for traffic problems."

Comment:

In the first example, attempts at self-justification do not bring the couple closer together in mutual understanding and harmony. They simply form a pattern of frustrating encounters around time negotiations which serves to alienate both partners. In the "right" response, the husband's pragmatic suggestion is received in a mature fashion by his wife. Had she refused his offer due to injured feelings, they may have had a very unpleasant encounter at the time of departure. Since she realizes that she is chronically late, she has thoughtfully permitted her husband to be independent of her in the matter of scheduled events. This shows true respect and concern for her spouse.

In the second example, the "wrong" wife discounts her husband's feelings, showing basic disrespect for him. Since she frequently fails to allow for contingencies in her time plans, she is frequently late. However, this wife makes it seem like it is her husband's problem rather than her's. The "right" wife acknowledges the fact that her own negligence, rather than circumstances, is responsible for her lateness, and her apology shows respect for her husband's feelings.

4. Do Not Interrupt Your Spouse

A woman may interrupt her husband for several reasons. After living with him for a while, she may feel that she knows how his sentence or speech is going to end, and so she cuts him short. It may be that she is overly eager to respond to his statement and doesn't let him finish; someone else in the family demands her attention and she responds to him instead; or he takes a very long time to say what he wants to say and she runs out of patience.

Interruptions include verbal interjections as well as physical maneuvers such as pulling faces, waving hands, getting up and walking around or out of the room, drumming fingers, and looking bored. All of these actions are disrespectful since everyone likes to have the opportunity for self-expression without disturbance. Many husbands have waited for the chance to grow up and leave their childhood table where they had to fight to get a word in edgewise. They look forward to the undivided attention of a doting wife and are keenly disappointed to find that they still have to compete to be heard.

Most wives would love to feel so relaxed and unhurried that they could just sit and gaze into the face of their beloved one. Instead, they find themselves in a pressured and rushed situation which leaves them feeling hurried a lot of the time. While their mate speaks, other things and people demand their attention. Is the soup boiling over while he talks about his day? Are three babies climbing up her leg when he asks her opinion about the upcoming visit of the in-laws? Is someone waiting for her to return a phone call when he wants to share an interesting thought with her? Unfortunately, wives may try to hurry the conversation along by interrupting because they cannot afford the luxury of allowing it to go at its own pace!

This excuse in no way lessens the harm done by interruptions, however. If a husband feels disrespected and unimportant because he is not attended to when he speaks, no valid "reason" can repair the damage. *Hashem* Himself allowed Avraham to have his say in asking for mercy for the people of Sodom. Although *Hashem* knew that Sodom lacked righteous people, He did not interrupt Avraham, but rather let him finish his plea. From this we learn that one must be careful to allow others to finish speaking.[17] Thus, a wife must find a way to carry on with her responsibilities and yet give her husband the attention he needs. How can she do this?

To begin with, she must learn that important little phrase, "excuse me." This phrase can be used to temporarily interrupt a discussion while something urgent is attended to (like that boiling pot or screaming child), yet it conveys the idea, "I'll be right back." Thus, its impact is quite different than if a woman suddenly averts her attention to another source without saying anything, just leaving her husband standing there with his mouth open!

Another technique that she can use is to become adept at stopping conversations before they start. If she sees that her husband wants to speak to her at an inconvenient moment, she can tell him that she is quite interested in what he has to say and will be available to discuss it at such and such a time (see Technique #1).

Once a conversation is underway, at the dinner table for example, a wife can endeavor to give undivided attention for as long as possible. Actually, she needn't be oblivious to other things going on around her (such as two children fighting or a baby spilling juice), but she can spread her attention discreetly. She can give as much eye contact as possible to her husband when things seem to be under control. Looking someone in the face is a powerful form of attention and makes them feel well heard. At other times, when not looking directly at him, she can nod her head in acknowledgment and respond verbally. Simultaneously she can give a child a determined stare, place her hand on someone's shoulder, bend over and pick up a dropped spoon, and so on. In other words, she indicates that she is still attending to her husband even while she is slightly occupied in other ways.

It is important that she does not permit the children to interrupt their father's speech, and she can teach them this concept directly by reminding them that Father is talking now. All of these actions on a wife's part serve to make her husband feel that he is indeed important enough to be listened to in his own home.

Sometimes, however, a husband has a style of monopolizing conversation, tending to ignore the needs of other family members. Such men enjoy talking for long periods and still expect to be listened to. How can a wife show this sort of husband the proper respect?

A wife can first attempt to communicate to her husband the fact that she (and the children) cannot really listen carefully for long periods of time. She needs to express this sincerely and politely, assuring him that she values his conversation highly. She should gently let him know when she can no longer attend by saying something like, "Yaakov, this is so interesting. I'd love to hear more about it later, but I've really got to do such and such right now." If he persists in making unreasonable demands on her attention, she must remain polite but firm. "I feel I can't carry on with my household responsibilities if I listen right now, and that gives me a sense of conflict which is uncomfortable." If even this sort of statement makes no impact, a wife must acknowledge to herself that her husband has a problem in this area. She is not obligated to behave in unnatural ways to accommodate his unhealthy pattern. If he gets extremely agitated as a result of being cut short, she may suggest some sort of marital counseling to help them negotiate this area of difficulty.

Example 1

wrong:

husband: "...so I need to decide whether we should buy the

mini-van or look at that station wagon tonight. *The van is cheaper, but it's five years old and...*"

wife: "Yes, I know, it's going to cost a fortune in repairs. So let's look at the wagon, since it's last year's model."

right:

husband: "...so I need to decide whether we should buy the mini-van or look at that station wagon tonight. *The van is cheaper, but it's five years old and I'm worried about the cost of repairs.*"

wife: "Excuse me, do you mind if I ask you a question about this?"

Example 2

wrong:

husband: "...so I asked him how long he thought it would take and..."

wife: "Yossi, did you finish off the milk this morning?"

right:

husband: "...so I asked him how long he thought it would take and he said about three months!"

wife: "Really! That's amazing. Oh, I just want to change the topic for a minute Yossi. Did you finish off the milk this morning? Miri is looking for some to have with her cookies."

Comment:

In the first example, the wife completes her husband's sentence. She is correct in her assessment of how he would finish his sentence, but she has not let him do it himself, thus depriving him of the satisfaction of completing his own thought. In the "right" dialogue, she waits until he has ended a sentence, although he has not completed his entire discussion. At this appropriate point, she politely checks with him to see whether he minds her interruption in his thought processes. He might say, "Please wait a minute," or he might say, "No I don't mind, go ahead." Whatever the outcome, the wife has shown respect for her husband and concern for his feelings. The slight difference in wording makes a big difference in marital harmony.

In the second example, the "wrong" wife interrupts her husband in midsentence to ask a question which has nothing to do with what he's talking about. This is sure to annoy him. It shows utter disrespect for what he's saying. If she really must interrupt his thought, she can do it as the "right" wife does, by first letting him finish his sentence, then commenting briefly on what he said, and then apologizing for the necessary interruption. These thoughtful words show him that she does respect him at least as much as she would respect any stranger who was speaking to her.

5. Use a Pleasant, Soft Tone of Voice

The Torah tells us that we are forbidden to hurt the feelings of others. "And you shall not hurt the feelings of one another, but you shall fear your Lord, for I God, am your Lord."[18] There are many ways to hurt a person's feelings (some of which will be discussed later), but one important source of pain is tone of voice. If someone shouts at you, you may feel insulted or terribly hurt. Imagine a husband screaming at his wife, "Be quiet already!" She will inevitably suffer as a result of his outburst.

Tone of voice can also inflict injury when it conveys sarcasm. "You want to start a business of your own? I don't believe it!" says a wife to her husband. Her dripping sarcasm can cut deeper than a knife, wounding his self-esteem and self-respect.

There are also less direct ways in which tone of voice causes pain. Mumbling rather than speaking up can create distance between marital partners, which hurts. Muttering, snarling, and other ways of indicating quiet anger also prevent closeness. The sound of a depressed, cold voice on the phone can weaken the marital bond. Even whining can distance spouses, since the sounds of constant complaint cause one to retreat from their source.

What is an appropriate tone of voice for a wife to use when speaking to her husband? The soft, pleasant tone used by airline stewardesses would be good. Professional tour guides, receptionists, waitresses, and other service people also know how to use a soft, kind tone. People can turn a lovely voice on when they're getting paid to do so! Wives are paid both in this world and in *olam ha'bah* for their efforts in this regard.

This does not mean, of course, that you have to sound phony to your own ears. It only means that you should take care to use YOUR OWN nice voice when speaking to your husband! Speak to him as if someone else is always around listening to you. (Someone is listening, after all.) Even if your own day has been frustrating or difficult, there is no need to snarl at your husband. A wife can even say, in a normal (not necessarily joyous) tone of voice, "I'm sorry I'm not in a good mood right now. I've had such a hard day." There is no need to scream the sentence, whine piteously, or otherwise speak rudely. One should take particular care to use an upbeat, cheery tone of voice when speaking on the phone, since tone of voice in this medium is of utmost importance. A husband

can get a clear message of rejection just from the tone of voice
he hears on the phone, even if the words themselves are
neutral. On the other hand, closeness and respect can be conveyed through the sound of a happy voice on the other end of
the receiver.

To check your own customary tone of voice, you can
leave a tape recorder on for a couple of hours (at dinner time,
perhaps). Another technique is to imagine what your husband
thinks of your voice when in your absence. Does he recall a
soft, loving tone, or does he hear a depressed, angry, or harried voice in his memory? You might even ask him! You can
ask the children as well. Of course, listening to yourself is the
best approach. Remember to aim for a soft and pleasant tone
when speaking to your spouse.

Example 1

wrong:

> husband: *"Aren't there any clean shirts here?"*
>
> wife (screaming): *"Have you ever thought of going to the
> laundry room and bringing them upstairs yourself? I'm over-
> worked, tired, and pregnant! You're lucky I got them washed
> today; if you want them brought upstairs, get me a maid!"*

right:

> husband: *"Aren't there any clean shirts here?"*
>
> wife (in a normal tone of voice): *"There are some in the laundry
> room."*

Comment:

When we use an escalated, angry tone of voice, it is easy
to get carried away. It is as if we are working ourselves up to

be good and mad. This is harder to do when we make a major effort to control the tone of voice we use. The Torah teaches us: "Accustom yourself to speak whatever you say in a pleasant tone of voice to each and every person at all times, and this will prevent you from getting angry."[19] Controlling tone of voice leads us to control our words as well, thus preventing us from becoming destructive and disrespectful in our interactions. Speaking in a pleasant tone helps us to remain pleasant and respectful in our dealings with our spouse.

6. Respect Your Husband's Competence

A wife may think of her husband as incompetent in some ways. In fact, since men and women have different abilities and inclinations, it is quite likely that he IS incompetent in some things according to HER standards. For example, many men seem to be incompetent (according to their wives!) when it comes to certain aspects of child care or household tasks. Even in the matter of business concerns, some wives feel that their husbands mismanage their affairs since they themselves would make a different set of decisions were they in the husband's place. All of these differences may lead a wife to disrespect her husband.

However, what seems to her to be incompetence is actually a different plane of functioning. Women are bestowed with a certain gift in the area of worldly affairs, and the Gemara itself advises men to follow their wives' advice in such matters, particularly regarding household management.[20] On the other hand, a man decides in spiritual matters.[21] A woman's ability in everyday functioning is a skill which is most useful in her responsibilities as a *balabusta*. Since *Hashem* created her to be a help to her husband, it is not surprising that she has the capacity to make life easier for him through her expertise in practical matters. She need not disrespect her husband because of his "incompetence" in her areas of competence. Rather, she can accept that his competence is simply of a different nature than hers.

For example, men are created with greater aggressive tendencies than women. All mothers are familiar with the differences between their little boys and little girls. A man who acquires a more peaceful nature through living a Jewish life style elevates himself as only a Jewish man can. This effort certainly demands a kind of competence, which Jewish women must respect. In fact, as a woman watches her husband being involved in mitzvah observance and the building of a Jewish home, she should remind herself that this is something very special. The *seforim* on her bookshelves, the Shabbos table in her dining room, the kosher food in her kitchen, and the little children in every room attest to her unique spiritual world. Her husband's goals permeate the home. There are women who would like to live a Jewish life but whose husbands are not interested. Naturally, their homes cannot radiate the level of spirituality that is attained when husband and wife work in partnership toward this goal. Thus a woman can include her husband's devotion to Yiddishkeit as part of his competence as a human being. He directs himself to lofty ideals.

On a practical level, men often demonstrate competencies in activities and skills that do not appeal to most women. Although it is clear that women can learn to do anything that men can do, women often lack interest in certain kinds of tasks and do not pursue them for that reason. Thus, while there is nothing stopping a woman from becoming an expert carpenter, plumber, or electrician, few wives care to develop these skills (there are exceptions, of course). Many, however, find that they have husbands who are willing to put energy into learning these kinds of things. As a group, men often have different interests than women do and therefore apply themselves in different directions. A wife can look at her own husband and observe how his areas of interest and competency differ from her own.

These differences imply that a woman should not EXPECT her husband to function as she does, since he is an entirely different creature. If he fails to show interest in or inclination for floor washing, for example, instead of making an issue of it, why not let it pass? Yes, he could certainly learn how if it was necessary for him to do so (and would even become proficient at it if it paid well enough!), but you could also learn how to do tasks for which you have little interest or inclination. Do YOU like to be forced to do things which you have little interest in or ability for? This is not to say that husbands should therefore be permanently excused from floor washing. It is only to say that if and when he does engage in this activity, you can be sure he won't do it like a woman does it! Although there are exceptions, most men do not do housework like women do. What happens when a woman needs her husband's household help? What if she is, Heaven forbid, ill or has just had a baby? Shouldn't he help out? Yes, of course! He should help his wife in any event, simply as an act of kindness and also to fulfill the commandment, "You shall certainly help him."[22] Nonetheless, the wife must accept this help without criticizing it for not being up to her standards.

Rather than being constantly frustrated over the fact that his performance is lacking, why not appreciate and respect the many things that he CAN do? Respect his competence in the areas in which he is competent.

Example 1

wrong:

> wife: "When you do the laundry, you can't leave the wet clothes in the washing machine for an hour and then put them in the dryer-you have to take them out as soon as the machine goes off. Furthermore, you should take the clothes out of the dryer promptly also, because things get wrinkled when you leave them there for too long."

> husband: "Look, I don't like all these complaints. If you don't like the way I do the laundry, I won't do it!"

Example 2

wrong:

> husband: "I need to get a new job. Things aren't working out for me at this place."

> wife: "You probably aren't going about it the right way. I bet you argue with everybody all day and your colleagues just don't enjoy working with you."

right:

> husband: "I need to get a new job. Things aren't working out for me at this place."

> wife: "Oh, I'm sorry to hear that. What's going wrong?"

Comment:

In the first example, although the wife is making valid complaints, she is not doing so in a constructive manner. Since it is the husband who is doing the laundry on this occasion, he must be left to do it without criticism. A basic rule is not to supervise your spouse in the performance of his tasks. (Do not make unsolicited suggestions regarding job performance, child rearing techniques, dishwashing skill, etc.) Criticism and complaints rarely lead to improved functioning, and they convey deep disrespect. If you don't like the way your husband cleaned the bathroom, you can either clean it yourself or hire someone to do it. Or, you can just accept the lower standard of shine and gleam.

The wife in this example needs to value her marriage more than her laundry. Let her wear wrinkled clothes for a bit, rewash them, or iron them later, while she waits for an opportunity to educate him about laundry in a positive way which enhances their relationship. For example, she can say one day, "Oh, the clothes were great today—no wrinkles! You must have taken them out of the washer and dryer really quickly, since that's what normally prevents wrinkles." To which he might respond, "Really? I never knew that. I wondered why the laundry didn't look right when I did it. Maybe that's the trick." Her patience in waiting for the right opportunity to present the information in a nonthreatening, nonintruding manner pays off in a harmonious relationship. She doesn't expect him to be naturally competent in the area of laundry skills, so she is not angry when she find he needs her help.

If a woman accepts that her husband's competencies lie in different areas from her own—that he is not a woman and doesn't function like one—she will be less frustrated with him. Moreover, she will be able to focus on his true competencies and appreciate and respect him for these. She should not endeavor to change him. Rather, she should assist him where necessary. Most of all, she should constantly remind herself of his special attributes and strengths and develop her gratitude for these.

In the second example, the "wrong" wife shows her obvious disrespect for her husband's abilities by assuming right away that he is being incompetent at work. This assumption may be valid, based on many past experiences. Nonetheless, when she shows her husband how little she thinks of him, she adds marital disharmony to his list of problems in life. If he really does have problems at work, he certainly doesn't need more at home. Let his wife show basic respect for him despite his human failings. Of course, if the wife has no reason to assume incompetency on her husband's part, her error is even more serious. Nonetheless, the consequences for marital happiness are the same, whether she has or hasn't valid reasons for suspecting that her husband is at fault. Her lack of support erodes marital respect and contentment.

7. Do Not Belittle Your Husband in Public

Earlier we learned that lack of support for a husband in a public situation may cause him to be shamed. There are many other ways to make a husband feel badly besides openly contradicting him. Some "innocent" little remarks can be quite hurtful and can therefore cause damage to a marriage. What is an "innocent" remark? It is the kind of statement which one makes to or about one's husband in public which, although said in a pleasant fashion, implies some sort of insult. For example, a wife watching her friend's husband bring in some tea for the guests might say, "Oh, is your husband ever sweet. My Hershel would never think to do that." Hershel, who is sitting there, may laugh in agreement, but he may also be embarrassed or uncomfortable. His wife has just spoken *lashon hora* about him in his presence and implied that he does not engage in thoughtful behaviors.

Offending people publicly is a grave sin.[23] The transgression is even worse if there are many who hear the *lashon hora*.[24] Moreover, we are forbidden to speak *lashon hora* in jest,[25] so even if a wife is "just joking" when she talks about her husband's behavior, she may be committing a serious *aveirah*. Thus, any public derogatory statement is to be avoided. If everyone is sitting around the Shabbos table and someone calls for a man to lead the *benching*, a wife should not say, "Don't let my Chaim do it—he can't sing at all!" Her remark serves no purpose other than to embarrass her husband. Unfortunately, people get into the habit of making this sort of casual "put down" and think that it has no impact on their marriage. However, no husband is immune to a public display of disrespect, and many, like King Achashverosh, have the urge to banish their wives because of this sort of behavior![26]

Example 1

wrong:

> hostess: "Here, Mr. Fatbush, have a second piece of cake."

> Mrs. Fatbush: "Oh, don't offer my husband more cake. He just doesn't know how to say no!"

right:

> hostess: "Here, Mr. Fatbush, have a second piece of cake."

> Mrs. Fatbush: (no comment)

Example 2

wrong:

> *husband (in a public situation): "Everyone around here is doing renovations. Maybe we should put an addition on our house too."*

> *wife: "The difference between you and everyone else, Yankele, is that they can afford it and you can't."*

right:

> *husband: "Everyone around here is doing renovations. Maybe we should put an addition on our house too."*

> *wife: "That's an interesting idea."*

Comment:

In the first example, although Mrs. Fatbush is obviously trying to be helpful at some level by preventing her husband from getting fatter, she is in fact insulting him. She is telling the hostess that he lacks will power. He surely experiences some level of humiliation or embarrassment from his wife's statement. Perhaps this would all be worthwhile if she could really prevent additional weight gain and its subsequent threats of heart disease, diabetes, or other illness. However, the additional 100 lbs. that her husband weighs has not yet been reduced by her "helpful" remarks, and he seems to eat just as he pleases when she's not around. Moreover, this particular scenario will likely end by the hostess exclaiming, "Don't be silly, Mrs. Fatbush. Let him enjoy his meal!" The second piece will be served and eaten and the "helpful" remark will leave no trace except a lingering aura of disrespect. It would be better if the wife made no comment at all. Even if her husband gains another pound, his blood pressure will at least not rise because of marital disharmony!

In the second example, the "wrong" wife makes a statement which is likely to embarrass her husband in a public
situation. In so doing, she is showing her obvious disrespect
for him, which causes further shame. Even if the remark is not
made maliciously, but rather, carelessly, its damaging effects
are the same. Better to do as the "right" wife does and make
light of his comment, not refuting it, but not taking it terribly
seriously. A matter like this shouldn't be decided in a public
setting in any event.

8. Respect Your Husband's Wishes

This may be one of the most important of all of the techniques of respect. Not paying attention to the desires and
wishes of one's spouse conveys utter disrespect. It says,
"What you want doesn't matter to me." Suppose your husband asks you to turn the volume down on the tape recorder.
If you tell him that the children like it loud, you are also telling
him that his wishes don't count. Although it is inevitable that
you will be unable to comply with his wishes at certain times,
whenever it is possible, you should do what he asks. Otherwise he gets the feeling that he is a "nothing"—a "nobody" in
his own home! If his requests are burdensome (he asks you to
make elaborate dinners seven days a week), you can explain
to him your limitations while assuring him that you will try to
please him as often as possible. Then you simply do what you
are able to comfortably do. You have no obligation to do what
you cannot do! If his requests are unreasonable (he asks that
you never leave the house), you can again explain your needs
and requirements while letting him know that you will accommodate his wishes as much as possible. If this is unsatisfac-

tory, you might seek the counsel of your Rav. In general, there is no need to develop peculiar or neurotic life styles in order to please your husband—rather, husband and wife should work together towards building a healthy and normal pattern of interaction.

Fortunately, most husbandly requests fall well within the normal range. Most husbands care for their wives sufficiently that they do not consciously wish to overburden them or make them unhappy in any way. Thus, when a husband asks a wife for anything—be it to sew on a button, bring him some tea, quiet the children down, invite guests over, or whatever— he is usually just letting her know what would make him happy or what would fulfill a particular need of his. This is an important form of communication. He doesn't have to start the sentence off with, "Do you know what would make me really happy right now?..." However, a wife might mentally insert that phrase in front of every request her husband makes. Then she can endeavor to show great respect for his wishes by doing what he asks if she is able to.

Example 1

wrong:

> husband: "Bayla, could you please call a few plumbers and get an estimate on the cost of repairing the water boiler? I won't have time to do it today."

> wife: "Do you think I have more time than you? I'm busy all day with car-pool, play-group, shopping, cooking, and a million errands. I certainly don't have time to sit on the phone for twenty minutes doing comparative pricing."

right:

> husband: "Bayla, could you please call a few plumbers and get

an estimate on the cost of repairing the water boiler? I won't have time to do it today."

wife: "I'm pretty booked up myself today, Yossi. I'll call one or two today, but I may not be able to do more until tomorrow. Can it wait another day?"

Example 2

wrong:

husband: "Sarah, would you try not to yell at the children so much? I find it most unpleasant to listen to."

wife: "Somebody's got to discipline them! That's how I do it."

right:

husband: "Sarah, would you try not to yell at the children so much? I find it most unpleasant to listen to."

wife: "I'm sorry, Chaim. I just lose control when they don't listen to me. I know it sounds awful, but I don't know how to get them to obey without screaming. I'll try not to yell if you tell me what I should do to get them to listen when I speak in a normal tone of voice."

Comment:

In the first example, the husband makes a request of his wife. The "wrong" wife lets him know rather rudely that she's too busy to do as he asks. This wife acts as if his reasonable request was burdensome and excessive. Since she does not indicate that she intends to try to fulfill it in any way, he is left feeling disregarded and unimportant. In the "right" dialogue, the wife shows that she is willing to do what she can for her husband while letting him know that she can't do the whole job unless she alters her plans significantly. She checks with him to see whether this is really necessary, making him feel that she takes his wishes quite seriously. Since this wife obviously tries to do what her husband asks of her, she fulfills the Sages' definition of "a proper woman" as one who "performs the will of her husband."[27] In other words, she tries to accommodate his wishes when they are reasonable and when it is not excessively difficult for her to do so.

In the second example, the "wrong" wife takes offence at her husband's request and replies defensively. In her retort, she shows no inclination to take his feelings into account, but on the contrary, makes it clear that she has no intention of changing her behavior. This kind of response can only detract from marital harmony. It demonstrates lack of respect for the wishes of her husband. The "right" wife, on the other hand, shows that she respects her husband's feelings and wishes when she indicates that she will try to change. She does ask for help, which is only reasonable. If her husband wishes her to change her behavior, he should be willing to help her do it. Her orientation is one of basic respect, conducive to building marital happiness.

9. Respect Your Husband's Individuality

Your husband is a unique human specimen. He has his own personal history, set of preferences, interests, inclinations, and potentials. Therefore, it is unreasonable to try and make him fit into your idea of what he "should" be rather than just let him be who and what he is. All women have some idea of what men "should" be like, however. They tend to try to push their husband toward this ideal mold so that they themselves will feel they have a "normal" spouse. For example, a woman might become exceedingly upset if her husband doesn't come home at 6:00 p.m. for dinner on weekdays because she thinks that all husbands are supposed to arrive at that time. Her four close friends tell her that their husbands are always home at 6:00, which adds to her disconcertment. Many arguments may ensue as she tries to convince her spouse that this is the hour at which he must arrive. Another wife becomes upset because her husband works on Sunday rather than taking the children on outings. She thinks that all husbands are available to relieve their wives for a few hours on Sunday and so has many heated disputes with her mate concerning why he can't also do this for her. A third wife sees that her friends' husbands take on second jobs in order to bring in a little more income. She wants her husband to try this as well. When he explains that he has different priorities, she becomes very agitated. Finally, there is the woman who complains that her husband never invites guests, but always leaves this up to her. Her own father always took the initiative in this area, bringing home *orchim* every Shabbos and making arrangements all the time. She thinks that all men do this and is impatient with her husband for being so passive in this regard.

All of these examples illustrate typical patterns of frustration stemming from the lack of acceptance of one's husband's individuality. In order to avoid such uncomfortable feelings, a wife must realize that her husband is entitled to be a separate person, unlike her relatives and friends. As long as he is not engaging in illegal or destructive behaviors, he may be himself in his own home. In fact, if she attempts to restrain him from doing what he likes to do, or pushes him to do what doesn't interest him, he will soon come to resent her. He will feel that she lacks respect for him and that she doesn't accept him.

Moreover, the truth is that each husband is a world unto himself (as is each wife). One will want to eat meat every night; another will want to avoid it even on Shabbos. One seems to utilize every moment of the day; another seems to have large amounts of "unproductive" time. One will go to bed early every night; another will be a "late owl." There is no use in hoping that your husband will be like everyone else's, because each husband is a complete individual.

Example 1

wrong:

> husband: "Do you mind if I listen to the ball game on the radio in here?"

> wife: "The ball game! Why do you have to waste your time with that nonsense? Nobody else wastes his time listening to that stuff-why do you have to? And anyway it gives me a headache, so I would really rather that you don't."

right:

> husband: "Do you mind if I listen to the ball game on the radio in here?"

> wife: "Yehudah, could you please take it into the other room so I could have quiet while I work?"

Example 2

wrong:

> husband: "I'd like to eat vegetarian meals on Shabbos in the summer. Meat is too heavy for me."

> wife: "Nobody does that, Shloimi! Everybody has regular cholent no matter how hot it is outside."

right:

> husband: *"I'd like to eat vegetarian meals on Shabbos in the summer. Meat is too heavy for me."*
>
> wife: *"I guess we could try that. I know you're supposed to eat the foods you enjoy on Shabbos. I might make some meat cholent as well, so the children and I can eat it if we want."*

Comment:

Although the wife in the first example is trying to encourage her husband to function at what she considers to be a more mature level, the end result is that she lowers him both in her own eyes and in his eyes. She shows her clear lack of acceptance of his tastes and preferences, implying that he is somehow deficient for liking what he likes. In fact, this man may spend most of his time in more serious activities, but simply enjoys an occasional diversion. Moreover, if she knew the truth, she would find that almost all of her friends' husbands also had some way of giving themselves a "break" from their daily routine—each finding his own particular outlet. Her fear that her husband's individuality makes him peculiar results in unnecessary anger and intolerance.

The "right" wife does not voice her concerns, but lets her husband be himself. Even if she objects to baseball games, she says nothing about it. She asks only that he listen in another room so that she doesn't have to hear it (although she phrases it more politely than that). In this way, she clearly respects her husband's individuality.

The "wrong" wife in the second example discounts her husband's wishes because she believes that "no one else" feels the way he does. Although this isn't true, even if it were, it would not be reason for her to ignore his individual preferences. Taste in food is a matter which is unique to each person and, as long as it falls within standards of kashrus and broad cultural norms, it really is an optional affair. Thus, the "right" wife doesn't make a fuss, but simply accepts her husband's wishes. She shows respect for his desires and for his uniqueness as a person.

So far we have discussed respect-developing strategies which pertain at all times in marriage. Now we will focus on the even greater challenge of maintaining respectful interactions during stressful situations in the relationship. Many of these techniques call for restraint—to simply refrain from speaking and acting disrespectfully, which permits the basic relationship to remain intact even while difficult negotiations are occurring.

It is important to note here that disagreements are an inevitable part of every marriage relationship. It would be impossible for two people of two different sexes, ages, backgrounds, and histories to be able to come to the identical conclusion on every single issue arising in the marital situation. Thus, there will always be differences of opinion. The challenge is to negotiate these differences in a respectful and loving manner. The existence of differences is no threat to a marriage; disagreements (even major disagreements) do not signal trouble in the relationship. They signal a need for communication efforts aimed at reconciliation and understanding. Even if many stormy years have already passed, it is never too late to learn the art of having respectful negotiations.

10. Do Not Negotiate in Front of Others

This technique is similar to previous ones which urge a wife to refrain from publicly embarrassing her husband. The difference is that it specifically refers to controversial conversations, rather than everyday chitchat. A controversial conversation is one in which husband and wife attempt to resolve some issue (this is referred to as "negotiating"). Any disagreement or dispute is considered an unresolved issue, as is any important decision. Thus, it would be inappropriate to have a public discussion with your husband about which schools the children should attend or whether or not you can afford a new vehicle. Similarly, one should not choose a public moment to offer constructive criticism to one's spouse or raise some point of contention. Even if someone else brings up an issue which is relevant to you and your husband, fight the temptation to join in the conversation! ("We also fight about money all the time because Reuven spends too much!") This may seem hard at the time, but it will certainly save you a very unpleasant scene when you are alone together and your husband lets you know just how he feels about your remarks!

Example 1

wrong:

> *husband: "Leah, do you want to rent a cottage with the Goldbergs this summer? They're all for it. Right, Moishe?"*

> *wife: "Simchah, how can you mention a cottage? You know you hate being alone during the week. Remember how I went away with the kids for just one week last year and you complained so bitterly when we got back! I didn't hear the end of it for months. Let's face it, you're not the 'weekend-husband' type."*

right:

> *husband: "Leah, do you want to rent a cottage with the Goldbergs this summer? They're all for it. Right, Moishe?"*

wife: "What an interesting idea! Let's talk about it on the weekend, O.K., Simchah?"

Example 2

wrong:

husband (in front of Shabbos guests): "Malkah, can the kids stay up a little later tonight? Maybe they want to come out with me."

wife: "You're too lenient with them, Asher. They should be in bed long before you leave. Now that you've mentioned your little outing, they're all upset because they can't go. If you wouldn't have said anything, they would never have known about it."

right:

husband: "Malkah, can the kids stay up a little later tonight? Maybe they want to come out with me."

wife: "Let's see how things go."

Comment:

In these dialogues, both husbands and wives have made a mistake. The husbands should not have invited public discussions of important decisions. The wives should have refrained from answering their queries, as they do in the "right" examples. Their answers surely would have embarrassed their husbands. The Sages said: "A person should rather have himself thrown into a fiery furnace, than put his fellow man to shame in public."[28] They understood the painful effects of public embarrassment. Certainly, a husband will feel distant from a wife who causes him this kind of discomfort. Since it is very difficult to discuss sensitive issues, such as differences of opinion and major decisions, without saying something which might prove embarrassing when heard by others, it is most important to keep all negotiations completely private.

11. Don't Mention Relatives

At any time, but particularly when you are involved in negotiations with your husband, it is wise to refrain from mentioning the subject of relatives. Of course, there are times when you will want to discuss your relatives—in the context of making arrangements to visit them, shop for them, assist them, and so on—but such conversations do not generally involve discussing relatives in terms of their personalities and characteristics. A person cannot be held responsible for the traits of his kin, and therefore it is most unfair to accuse one's husband of having the same faults as any of his relatives. For example, a wife might be tempted to point out that her husband is as stingy as his father. Such a statement would have many problems inherent in it—for example, the use of labeling, judging, exaggerating, personalizing, and comparing (all of which will be discussed later). The mention of the bad character trait of one's husband is certainly destructive enough without adding destructive elements by mentioning the character of the father-in-law. It is forbidden to speak *lashon hora* about relatives, including parents, brothers, sisters, uncles, aunts, and cousins.[29] Even though the father-in-law may be a stingy person, it is *lashon hora* to make mention of this. Thus, the statement is forbidden on this basis alone. However, a wife would refrain from making such statements even if she realized their destructive impact only on her marriage.

What is so destructive about mentioning relatives? To

begin with, a person feels attached to his relatives even if he himself doesn't approve of them or like them. People take offence if their relatives are insulted. Secondly, when relatives are mentioned in the context of a disagreement or dispute, it is generally in a negative connotation. The relative is mentioned as the epitome of some negative *middah*. The husband thus experiences a double "put-down"—one for his own insult and one for the insult of his relative. Because many people have an extra sensitivity regarding their close relatives, insults involving these people hurt even more than "normal" insults. Of course, a wife is aware of the increased hurt-value of mentioning relatives, and that is why she chooses this technique in the heat of anger. She must be aware, however, that after her anger has subsided, the pain of such insults lingers and erodes the basis of respect in the relationship. *Lashon hora* hurts the wife, her husband, and the relative spoken about. It should be avoided in all negotiations.

Example 1

wrong:

> *wife: "Every time we leave your parents' house, I notice you start acting like your dad–cold and aloof. I really don't like it."*

right:

> *wife: "I notice that you're a little tense after we leave your parents' house. Do you notice it too? Is there something I can do to help you be more relaxed after a visit?"*

Example 2

wrong:

> *wife: "You're emotionally cold just like the rest of your family. None of you knows how to show affection in a normal way. I don't know why I didn't notice it before I married you."*

right:

> *wife: "I need more demonstrations of affection from you. Maybe I'm insecure, but I just need it. What can we do about it?"*

Comment:

In the first example, the "right" wife finds a way to express her feelings without resorting to *lashon hora* about relatives. The tone of her comment is quite different from that in the "wrong" example, where she sounds like she is inviting a fight rather than trying to be helpful. Her allusion to her father-in-law serves as an aggravating provocation, providing no constructive purpose, but adding many destructive overtones. She fails in her goal to negotiate respectfully as long as she insists on mentioning relatives.

Similarly, in the second example, the "right" wife finds a way to make a sincere statement of complaint without adding insults about her husband and his family. In this way she maintains respectful negotiations and is much more likely to get what she wants from her husband. If she antagonizes him with nasty remarks about his family, however, she will reap only conflict and ill feelings. Her goal of improving the situation will not be met in this fashion.

12. Respect Your Husband's Right To Complain

Allowing your marriage partner to make a complaint to you is a form of respect. The message is, "You have a right to your thoughts and feelings and I'm interested in what you have to say." On the other hand, not permitting your husband to issue a complaint gives the opposite message, "Since you're not perfect, don't tell me what's wrong with me. I don't want to hear your thoughts and feelings." Suppose your husband complains that you never take his suits to the cleaners early enough in the week. Your job would be to respond to his complaint—to accept it by listening carefully, acknowledging that you heard it, and discussing possible solutions. NEVER CHANGE THE SUBJECT. Don't say, "Well, you never pick up milk when I ask you to." If your husband's complaint reminds you of a complaint that you want to mention, make a mental note to bring up your issue at the next opportunity, but no sooner than two hours after your husband's complaint. After all, you have the whole year to make any complaints that you would like to make; you don't have to choose THIS particular moment when your husband has something to tell you, and it is most disrespectful to do so.

Example 1

wrong:

> husband: *"I think you're too lenient with the children."*
>
> wife: *"Well, I think you're too strict with them."*

right:

> husband: *"I think you're too lenient with the children."*
>
> wife: *"You think I need to be firmer with them?"*
>
> husband: *"Yes. You let them get away with too much."*
>
> wife: *"Could you give me some specific examples and tell me what you think I should have done instead of what I did? That would be helpful to me. You could be right about this."*

Example 2

wrong:

> *husband: "Why are there never any clean socks in my drawer?"*
>
> *wife: "Why does my broken tap never get repaired?"*

right:

> *husband: "Why are there never any clean socks in my drawer?"*
>
> *wife: "I didn't realize there was a problem. I'm washing every-thing I find in the laundry basket. Maybe you need to buy some new socks."*

Comment:

In the first example, the "wrong" wife acts defensively, offering a counter accusation to her husband's complaint. This is a natural instinct that many people have in their attempt to preserve their self-esteem. They feel that a criticism threatens their acceptability. However, this is far from the truth. Rebuke can be a demonstration of caring since the one who offers it obviously hopes to provide education or improvement in some way. *Hashem* Himself offers rebuke to His people when necessary, and we receive it as an indication of His love for us.[30] If a husband offers criticism, we should assume that he does so in order to yield some improvement, not that he is maliciously trying to hurt us. It is essential that a wife judge her husband favorably[31] and assume that his intentions are positive.

The "right" wife accepts the complaint by listening and telling her husband what she heard him say. This is a very impor-

tant step in the process of communication. It is often referred
to as giving "feedback." Essentially, the listener paraphrases
what was said and indicates whether or not he or she understood the message. The wife does this and goes on to ask her
husband for more information. Ideally, she will listen to everything he has to say on the subject until she understands his
point of view thoroughly. Then she will respond with her own
thoughts and feelings on the matter, and they will work toward
some mutually satisfying solutions. The conversation will not
be a battle of wills fought by two adversaries, but rather a
process of negotiation aimed at increasing marital harmony
and respect.

In the second example, the "wrong" wife changes the subject when her husband makes a complaint. He talks about
socks and she talks about taps. Since they are not discussing
the same subject, there is no hope of proper conflict resolution. Instead, the couple will antagonize each other as each
tries to make his or her own point. This is not the appropriate
moment for this wife to complain about her broken tap. It is
unfair of her to answer his criticism with her own complaint. It
shows disrespect for his right to complain and disrespect for
his feelings. This kind of treatment creates distance between
marital partners, rather than closeness and understanding.

13. Talk About Issues, Not Personalities

The Torah prohibits insulting people or hurting them with
our words.[32] When husband and wife are engaged in negotiations, they must therefore learn to discuss only the subject at
hand while refraining from discussing personalities. For example, suppose a wife complains that her husband forgets to

take the garbage out every week. She must rush out early in the morning before the refuse truck arrives and carry the heavy bags to the roadside. Since her husband accepted the task of taking out the garbage, she is extremely annoyed that he does not fulfill his responsibility in this area. When she rebukes him, however, she must be very careful not to insult him. She may be tempted to label him as inconsiderate, thoughtless, or lazy. Since these insults show disrespect and cause emotional pain, she may be committing two Torah transgressions. Moreover, name-calling of this sort will never help to resolve an issue.

When personality is discussed rather than the subject, nothing is accomplished except marital distress. If she really would like him to assume responsibility for the task of taking out the garbage, she should talk about their original agreement, the effect that his negligence has on her, ideas for solutions to the problem, and any other subject-related issue. She should avoid talking about his character and *middos*. This also means that she should avoid "psychoanalyzing" him. In other words, she should not delve into his motivations ("If you really cared about me and how I felt, you would have taken the garbage out") or put words into his mouth ("When you don't take the garbage out, it's your way of telling me you don't like to help out around here"). Looking for reasons for unacceptable behavior does nothing to bring a couple closer together, but it can certainly contribute to whatever distancing they are experiencing. In order to make things go the way you'd like them to go, you should focus on describing your wishes and your ideas for implementing them ("I'd like you to take out the garbage when you say you will, and I'm willing to remind you once on the appropriate evenings if you want me to"). Always stay on topic and oriented toward the future rather than the past. The question you should be asking yourself is, "What can we do to solve this problem?" Don't ask, "Why doesn't he behave differently?"

Example 1

wrong:

> *wife:* "*I think it's really unfair of you to keep me and the children waiting on the corner for half an hour after you said you'd pick us up. It was cold outside and they were whining the whole time. You're really inconsiderate sometimes. If you weren't so self-centered, I'm sure you would have stopped what you were doing and come when it was time to come!*"

right:

> *wife:* "*You know, the children and I had to wait outside in the cold for half an hour till you arrived. They were whining the whole time and I was very distressed. I was worried about what could have detained you, and I was having trouble calming the kids down. What can we do to make sure this sort of thing doesn't happen again?*"

Example 2

wrong:

> *wife:* "*You are too stingy. We can afford a new sofa, but you just want to hoard our money. You're being unreasonable. Why should I have to look at and sit on our old ugly couch every day when we can easily get something practical and attractive now? You don't care about how I feel.*"

right:

> *wife:* "*I feel we can afford a new sofa now. The old one is unattractive and uncomfortable. I would really enjoy having something pretty and practical in our living room–it would make*

me really happy. Maybe we could go over the budget together and see if we can manage the expense."

Comment:

The name-calling in the "wrong" examples does nothing toward getting the problem resolved, but does a lot toward antagonizing the husband. The wife should practice leaving out the word "you" in her complaints. The emphasis should be on "I" as the wife states her own feelings and reactions. In any complaint, the complaining person should make a statement of how an issue affects her. She can use any set of feeling words to describe her emotions: "I feel upset," "I am uncomfortable," "I'm feeling troubled," "I was very worried," "I'm not happy," and so on. All labels should be avoided in the course of the discussion. Labels are summarizing words like "thoughtless," "selfish," "immature," "lazy," or "mean". It is much better to use extra words to avoid the use of destructive labels. For example, a wife might say, "Perhaps you didn't realize how I would feel in such circumstances" rather than saying, "You were totally thoughtless." The Torah itself uses this technique in order to avoid unpleasant language (e.g., saying, "And of every animal which is not clean" rather than saying "unclean animals.")[33] A person should likewise avoid using disgusting language, for this practice can harm him.[34] It also damages relationships due to the inherent disrespect.

Careful language conveys deep respect, whereas careless language can convey the deepest disrespect, verging on or including hateful feelings. The pain caused in negotiations involving verbal abuse lingers on long after the particular issue has been resolved. Words cannot be retrieved. The tongue can be as dangerous as a sharp knife.[35] Verbal abuse cannot occur when a person resolves not to discuss personalities, but only to stay on topic with an issue. If a woman is so upset that she can't talk rationally about the issue at that time, she can make a sincere, powerful statement of her feelings without using destructive language. For example, she might say, "I'm really too upset right now to talk about this. I feel like screaming! I'm going to my room to calm down, and then I'll want to discuss this with you afterwards." It would be perfectly clear to her husband that she was intensely upset, and yet she would have said nothing that could be construed as destructive to their relationship or hurtful to him. Obviously, such careful speech requires the use of self-control, but all of us are capable of learning to use that control if we choose to.[36] Even extreme emotions do not interfere with our ability to control our speech and actions. There is never an excuse for a disrespectful, destructive outburst.

14. Speak Quietly

When negotiating, it is important to speak quietly. We have discussed tone of voice during regular conversations, emphasizing the importance of using a pleasant, everyday voice. During confrontations, however, it is of particularly great importance to speak in civil tones. Shouting is a very destructive technique demonstrating total lack of respect. It is highly unpleasant to be in the presence of someone who is screaming, ranting, and raving, and it does nothing to increase affection and understanding. Anger often leads one to irrational, self-defeating behaviors, whereas "the wisest course of action is to be quiet at the moment of anger or anguish."[37] When you want to influence someone to change for the better, it is essential to remain calm and speak pleasantly. Only this way will your words be effective.[38]

If yelling is so counterproductive and destructive, why do so many people do it? People erroneously feel that they will be heard better if they raise their voice. A wife might think, "Since he is not responding properly when I speak in a normal tone of voice, I'll try shouting to see if that helps." Many times a woman will feel that her statement lacks power unless it is shouted. She feels that her husband will pay greater attention if she shows him how distraught she is. However, her own aroused state is an open invitation to the *yetzer hara* to lead her to greater folly and harm. Each word spoken loudly feeds into her own rage, causing her to escalate further.

No rational, problem-solving conversation can be carried on when people are shouting. Only pain and distance are created under such circumstances. Thus, once a woman sees that she is engaged in a shouting match, her best course of action is to withdraw from the conversation, to calm down, and to make an appointment to discuss the issue at a later point. This could be later that same day, or it could be a day or two afterwards. There is no need to delay sleep until every issue is resolved. Neither is there a need to hold on to angry feelings just because one issue needs negotiation. The marriage is not "on-hold" every time an issue needs resolution; all the positive aspects of the relationship continue to exist, and one can continue to love one's spouse even while in the middle of working out a particular problem. If one focuses on problem-solving rather than on emotional issues and personalities, the whole business of arriving at solutions becomes a much calmer and more logical affair. Speaking quietly helps to avoid the escalation and anger which deter one from effective problem-solving.

Example

wrong:

> *wife (shouting): "I can't stand this mess! Nobody around here helps me at all! And you, Shmuel, you set a terrible example for the children by sitting around and watching me slave away; I'm sick of it!"*

right:

> *wife (waits until she's not upset and then says): "I feel I need more household help. Since we can't afford a live-in, each member of the family will have to do a little more. Shmuel, can you help me draw up a list of chores and set up a system for their division for everyone in the family?"*

Comment:

In the "wrong" example, the husband will see that his wife is upset. He will also feel rejected and unhappy in her presence. It is doubtful that her tirade will result in increased cooperation from the members of her household, however. More likely, everyone will feel miserable for a while, but will continue in their normal ways. Her husband, observing her irrational tantrum, will either assume that it's "that time of the month" or that she's just having one of her usual "fits." In either case, he will not be inclined to take her seriously.

In the "right" example, the wife has chosen to speak when she is feeling more calm. Perhaps she had looked around at the mess in the house, felt like screaming, decided to say nothing at the time, and waited until she felt able to discuss the problem rationally. When she finally speaks, her tone of voice is quiet, her words are well-considered, and she is focused on solving the problem. Because of this, she will likely be well-attended, and she stands a good chance of resolving an important issue. Most importantly, *shalom bayis* is maintained and respect permeates the marital negotiations.

15. Only Mention One Issue at a Time

When you have a complaint to raise, it is important to stay on topic with it. Don't be tempted to "throw in the kitchen sink" when you find that you've finally got an audience! Mentioning more than one issue at a time tends to result in an overload of criticism. A husband may be able to respond effectively to one complaint, but if three more are hurled at him he will simply feel attacked and will lose any motivation to engage in sincere problem-solving. Thus, it is essential to decide what issue you want to negotiate and make sure that you discuss only that one issue.

Example 1

wrong:

> *wife:* "Hershel, I don't think you were very sociable towards our guests today."
>
> *husband:* "I'm sorry. I had a bad headache."
>
> *wife:* "You always have a headache. If it's not that, then it's a stomach ache."
>
> *husband:* "Well, I'm under a lot of tension lately, so I guess it comes out that way."
>
> *wife:* "You wouldn't be under so much tension if you would just learn to manage your business better. I don't understand why you don't accept Mr. Horowitz's offer to consult with him about your financial problems."

right:

> *wife:* *"Hershel, I don't think you were very sociable towards our guests today."*
>
> *husband:* *"I'm sorry. I had a bad headache."*
>
> *wife:* *"Oh, I'm sorry to hear that. But it's really not fair to our guests to be curt with them. I only hope they weren't offended or hurt. What do you think can be done in case you're not feeling well and we've already invited people over? Do you have any ideas?"*

Example 2

wrong:

> *wife:* *"Zvi, could you please rinse your dish out when you've finished with it instead of leaving it on the counter? And could you put your shoes back in the cupboard instead of leaving them in the middle of the floor? By the way, when are you planning to rake up those leaves in the front yard? Oh, I also forgot to tell you yesterday that our neighbor complained about that mess of newspapers you've left at the side of the house."*

Comment:

Staying on topic makes it possible to fully resolve an issue. However, flitting from one subject to the next ensures that no problem will be solved. Moreover, the emotional impact is one of rejection and disrespect. Nobody likes to hear so many complaints in one sitting! In the first example, the "right" wife carefully steers herself back toward the issue at hand, enabling the husband to respond and engage in finding a solution. In the second example, the wife is making so many complaints that her husband is sure to ignore all of them and feel very annoyed with her. It would be much better if she mentioned only one of the issues on her list. They are probably not equally important. She should set priorities in her mind, selecting the most serious complaint to mention and refraining from mentioning the others at that time or perhaps ever. Such a barrage of criticism conveys disrespect and creates marital tension.

16. Keep It Short

Nobody likes to listen to a lecture. When you start to lecture, your husband stops listening (and so do your children!). When you have a complaint to make or an issue to raise, find the shortest way possible to phrase your statement. State the problem at hand and issue an invitation for problem-solving. This should take approximately two to three sentences.

A lecture, on the other hand, is a full-blown speech laden with examples and explanations. The assumption behind a lecture is that the listener requires a lot of information and that repetition and redundancy will be effective in communicating an important point. However, in all likelihood your husband already has a good idea about how you feel about most issues, and he does not need you to start from scratch to explain all your thoughts and feelings. This is certainly true if you are discussing an "old" issue—one that has been negotiated previously. It is also true for most newer issues because a particular problem will reflect a general attitude that you hold (and have probably expressed before). Moreover, when excess information is given at a time of rebuke, people have a natural tendency to withdraw defensively. The more you say, the stronger this reaction becomes in your husband, who may be feeling, "All right, already! Enough already! I get the idea—stop picking on me!"

Brevity has more power because you evoke less defensive barriers in your husband. He is still receptive to your words and is emotionally free to respond to your point. Thus, the shorter your statement, the more powerful a communication tool it is.

Example

wrong:

> wife: "Shloimi, I really need your help in getting the children ready for bed. Why can't you bathe the little ones for me while I finish off in the kitchen or help the others with their homework? After dinner, you just relax for an hour while I run around like a maniac trying to do everything by myself! It really isn't right, you know. I'm exhausted by the time I get them tucked in. One person shouldn't have to do everything alone—it's not like you're particularly busy at that time of day, is it? I know you need to relax a bit, but what about me? Don't I deserve a break too? If you'd just help with one thing, the whole operation would be speeded up immensely. I really can't carry on like this."

right:

> wife: "Shloimi, could you take on the job of bathing the younger kids after dinner time? It would help me out a lot."

Comment:

In the "right" example, it is quite likely that the husband will respond to his wife's question in a reasonable manner. He will either explain why he can't do what she asks, or he will agree to do it. The focus of the conversation is on negotiation. In the "wrong" example, the wife's lengthy speech invites emotional defensiveness in her husband. If he remembers what her question is, he will likely retort in a negative manner. His impression will be that she is attacking him unreasonably, and he will search for self-defensive replies in response. If we look carefully, we see that no new crucial information is relayed in the extra words—the main point is that she needs help. This idea can be expressed quite briefly (as is done in the "right" example). The extra words only serve to antagonize and convey lack of respect. Their impact is thus destructive rather than constructive. The wife needs to develop the art of NOT speaking in order to be a better communicator in marriage.

17. Don't Nag

Nagging involves repeating one's request many times. Usually a wife nags because her husband doesn't respond to her first few statements. For example, a wife has asked her husband to spend some time helping one of their boys with his homework, and he has agreed to do so. Several days go by, yet he has not sat down with the child. She repeats her request. He apologizes for forgetting and agrees to do it at the next opportunity. This opportunity doesn't arrive; several more days pass and no studying has occurred. The wife approaches her husband a third time, with increased agitation now. He responds impatiently as well, claiming that it has been a busy week and he just hasn't been able to do it. Another week passes and the wife decides to raise the issue again. Now the husband is really annoyed and insists that she stop nagging him about this issue!

It is true that nagging conveys disrespect. The message given is, "I don't trust you to do your part. I have to keep reminding you as if you were a wayward child." However, a husband who agrees to do something and doesn't do it is, in fact, acting like a wayward child. Nonetheless, it is essential that a wife refrain from playing a destructive mothering game with her spouse. He doesn't want another mother and she certainly doesn't want to be one. How do they avoid this sort of negative interaction?

There are several answers to this question, depending on the nature of the nagging pattern. We will examine each separately.

1) A wife may nag her husband to do something he's supposed to do for himself.

Examples of this kind of situation are when a wife repeatedly tells her husband that he should clean off his desk so it will be more organized, or she reminds him to do more exercise. In these cases, the wife is attempting to help her husband do what he is supposed to do, but her help becomes a source of friction in the relationship. The solution to nagging of this sort is as follows: a) She can remind him ONCE about what he has to do, providing that he has agreed that he wants her to do this.

b) She refuses to remind him a second time, even if he insists that he wants her to. She can explain to him (once) that it is unpleasant for both of them when she works too hard at getting him to do something that is plainly his own responsibility. If, as a result of her lack of urging, he does not tidy his desk or do his exercise, she must realize that in the long run she is actually helping him to take responsibility for his affairs. It may take a while, but eventually he will realize that these things are up to him and that if he wants to succeed at them, he will have to do so by himself. *Shalom bayis* is maintained, because she has refused his invitation to nag (remind him more times).

Moreover, her lack of nagging conveys a basic acceptance of him as he is, and this, too, contributes to *shalom bayis*.

2) A wife may nag her husband to do something for her or the household.

If the wife finds herself repeatedly asking her husband to do a certain task (take out the garbage, pay the bills, fix the broken door, learn with a child, etc.), then she should

a) Ask him to do the task ONCE.

b) If she sees he hasn't done it after a reasonable amount of time, she should choose an appropriate private moment to sit down with him, make good eye contact, tell him earnestly that the particular task is important to her for whatever reason, ask him what will enable him to do it promptly (she should not agree to remind him a second time), and let him know very warmly how much she appreciates his efforts in this matter.

c) It would be optional for the couple to arrange some reward/punishment system if they felt it would be useful. For example, the husband might agree to do the dishes for a week if he forgets to take out the garbage on Monday night. A reward for doing a task could be any pleasant reinforcement such as a special dinner or dessert, a special time together, a small gift that you wouldn't otherwise purchase, or a special favor from you. The rewards and punishments should be suggested by the husband. This system should only be used if it appeals to him.

d) If all of this still fails to move your husband to fulfill his responsibility to you, you can let him know that you feel it is time to hire or purchase the service in question. For example, if he just can't seem to sit down to help your son with his schoolwork, you suggest that a tutor should be arranged. If he can't seem to get around to fixing the broken door, you suggest that a handyman should be called in. If he should react extremely negatively to these kinds of solutions, you can suggest that you and he go to your Rav or counselor to get a third opinion. If that suggestion results in even stronger negativity, evaluate how important the issue actually is. If you decide that life can go on without the particular job being done, then accept that it won't be done and don't mention it again. If it is something very essential (he refuses to seek *parnasah* and you are going hungry), then seek counseling alone.

Example

wrong:

> *wife:* "Chaim, could you please hang up your coat in the cupboard when you come in?"

> *husband:* "Sorry, I'll get it in a moment."

> *wife (after ten minutes):* "Chaim, your coat is still on the chair!"

> *husband:* "I'll be right there."

> *wife (after another twenty minutes):* "Honestly, Chaim! How many times do I have to ask you to hang up your coat? You're worse than the children!"

right:

> *wife:* "Chaim could you please hang up your coat in the cupboard when you come in?

> *husband:* "Sorry, I'll get it in a moment."

> *wife (after ten minutes hangs it up herself; later that night she says):* "Chaim, you generally leave your coat on the chair when you arrive and I generally put it in the cupboard for you. Have you noticed that? You know, that means one extra thing for

*me to do in the day, and as I am already fully occupied picking
up after the children, it just drains me to have to pick up your
things too. Do you have any suggestions that would help you
to remember to put your own coat on a hanger? I would really
appreciate your help in this area. "*

Comment:

Although this is a simple example, it is actually possible for
a wife to spend ten or twenty years nagging her husband to
hang up his coat. The unpleasant interaction destroys some of
the marital harmony and happiness that the couple could
otherwise enjoy. If the wife chooses to let her husband know
how she feels about this minor irritation, she has a chance that
he will respond to her sincere plea out of his concern for her.
On the other hand, there are some husbands who, although
they love their wives, simply cannot or will not look after their
own physical needs. It may be that their childhood training
yielded this result or that they have so many other things on
their minds that they expect their wives to handle this area of
life for them. Whatever the reason, if it turns out that the husband does not begin to hang up his coat, the wife can evaluate
how much of a problem this is for her. If it is one of too many
things that she has to do for him, perhaps counseling is in
order. If, however, he is not otherwise unreasonable or
demanding, perhaps she will just decide to hang up his coat for
the duration of their marriage. Once she makes this decision,
she no longer has to ask him every day to do this task. She will
simply do it for him. She has made this decision, not as a martyr who has no other choice, but as a loving wife who has
decided that *shalom bayis* is more important than the minor
inconvenience of hanging up a coat. If she really harbors

resentment, however, it would be better to attempt further negotiation with or without a counselor.

18. Interpret Your Husband's Behavior Positively

The Torah urges us to judge our fellow man positively.[39] This halachah pertains to one's husband particularly, as do all the halachos bein adam le'chavero (between people). It is in the context of our intimate relationships that we are judged in this realm. Moreover, we learn that as we judge others, so Hashem judges us—that is, when we are lenient and favorable in our assessment of people, so Hashem will be lenient and favorable in His assessment of us.[40] The challenge is to be able to judge one's husband positively when in the midst of a confrontation or dispute of some kind. Such judgment prevents escalation and hurtful negotiations, removing the assault to one's self-esteem.[41]

When a husband says something unfair or provocative, such as an insult or harsh accusation, a wife's lenient judgment can prevent a painful and destructive interaction. She can say to herself, "He's under a lot of stress right now. He doesn't mean what he's saying," or "He doesn't know how to express his anger constructively; we can work on this together—I know he'll improve." With such thoughts in mind, her response to his outburst will be tempered and reasonable. On the other hand, she can say to herself, "He's cruel and horrid. His only wish is to hurt me," or "He's completely irrational and unfair. He doesn't care about me at all." If she thinks like this, her harsh judgment harms both her husband and herself. She will internalize the pain caused by her own negative assumptions, and she will likely lash out against him in response to his outburst. This will lead to increasingly destructive interactions, harmful to the marriage itself.

When a wife learns to judge her husband positively, she will be much more able to respond to abuse in the proper manner. Although her husband's provocation "entitles" her to retort in a hostile fashion, it is like receiving one free ticket to Siberia. Who wants to be out in the cold? If the wife accepts this "ticket," then she has the short-term satisfaction of hitting back, but the pain and distance only boomerangs home. She succeeds in enlarging the gulf between herself and her husband. On the other hand, if she chooses to judge her husband positively and consciously refrains from attacking him in retaliation, she creates the possibility of quick reconciliation. This is the ideal both from a matrimonial point of view and from a spiritual point of view. The Torah gives much praise to those who are able to remain silent in the face of insults.[42] In fact, it is in the merit of those who do not respond to abuse that the world is sustained![43] Thus the wife can be sure that she is doing the right thing by not responding in kind to her husband's provocations. (She might also keep in mind that any pain she suffers as a result of his accusations can atone for her own transgressions.[44] Concentrating on such a thought can help her to restrain herself and to appreciate that everything comes from *Hashem*—even the insult she is now suffering.)

Silence in the face of insults does not refer only to the literal absence of response, but also to lack of rebuttal. Essentially, when offered an "invitation to fight" the wife declines the invitation.[45] Thus, if faced with an unfair communication strategy from her husband, a wife can respond in many "fair" ways. Her first thought needs to be some kind of positive judgment of the situation ("He doesn't mean what he's saying") so that she can become more objective and less subjective about the experience at hand. In an objective mode, she can see that her husband is transgressing rules of healthy communication and probably halachic rules as well (if he is trying to hurt her feelings in any way). She identifies that this reflects a problem that HE is having. She then tries to help him to express himself in more permitted and more constructive ways. She can do this by letting him know that she understands how upset he is. She can give him feedback as to what his complaint seems to be, indicating that she hears and comprehends it.

If he is truly agitated, she should attempt to delay actual problem-solving until a calmer moment. She could say, "Since we're upset right now, why don't we leave this discussion for a while and meet again around 9:00 tonight. I'm sure we'll be able to work things out then." She should not say, "Since YOU'RE so upset right now..." since that will only increase his anger. Even if she herself is perfectly calm, she should phrase this comment as "we" or even "I" in order to lessen his defensiveness. She should never walk out of the room or slam the door on him as a way of keeping silent! She must always get his agreement to postponement of the discussion. If he won't agree, she can listen passively as long as he wants an audience. She needn't respond to anything at that time.

If he is not too emotional, she can continue to help him express his thoughts and feelings by helping him to focus on problem-solving ("So what do you think we should do about this?"). If it seems he wants to release pent-up emotions, she can help him to do so less destructively by asking him to phrase things differently and showing him clearly that she hears what he is saying. She agrees with him where possible, apologizes where appropriate, and empathizes when she can. She needn't defend herself or even explain her side of the story at this point. When he is no longer upset, later that day or the next, she can invite him for a follow-up discussion to resolve further issues. At this point, she can explain her own perceptions and thought processes and engage in constructive negotiation.

Example 1

wrong:

> husband: *"Malky, I am sick and tired of this mess around here! You must be the worst housekeeper in North America!"*

> wife (thinking that he's insensitive and cruel): *"If that's the way you feel, then you can go find yourself another housekeeper!"*

right:

> husband: *"Malky, I am sick and tired of this mess around here! You must be the worst housekeeper in North America!"*

> wife (thinking that he's in a really bad mood and is not being careful about his speech): *"You seem really upset, Yaakov. Is the mess really bothering you or is something else on your mind?"*

> husband: *"Nothing's on my mind–I'm just sick of walking into this disaster area at the end of a hard day, that's all."*

> wife: *"Oh, you can't stand this chaos when you get home?"*

> husband: *"That's right. And I don't know what it is that you do all day that you're so busy you can't clean this place up."*

> wife: *"I see. You think I should be able to do better. Well, I'd be willing to sit down with you and discuss this further. Could we meet after dinner tonight when the kids are sleeping and talk about this some more?"*

> husband: *"Fine. Because I want to solve this once and for all."*

Example 2

wrong:

> husband: "Hadassah, where did you hide my blue tie?"

> wife (assuming that he's intentionally provoking her): "In the garbage can."

right:

> husband: "Hadassah, where did you hide my blue tie?"

> wife (assuming that he is making an error in communication techniques): "It's probably hanging on the tie rack in the cupboard. Eli, I would appreciate it if you wouldn't suggest that I "hide" your things when you can't find them. It implies a nasty intent on my part which I don't have and don't like being accused of having."

Comment:

In the first example, the wife's negative judgment of her husband leads her to respond most disrespectfully to him. Of course, he invited such a response by his own disrespectful style of communication. Now, however, they are on a spiral of destructive emotions and are likely to hurt each other severely rather than solve any problem they have. Since the wife took her husband's inappropriate remarks to heart, she adds her own "bundle of wood to the fire" and invites him to be increasingly abusive. Each of his remarks will escalate with increased fury and abuse.

The "right" wife assumes that her husband's behavior is not indicative of his true feelings, but rather indicates some stress he is under or some mistake he is making. Thus, feeling unthreatened by his tirade, she is able to listen to him without attempting to defend herself. She realizes that he is extremely upset at this moment and that it would be futile to actually try to resolve the issue right then. However, she does not try to cut him short, but allows him to "let off some steam" for a few minutes, showing him that she is listening to what he has to say. Although he continues to be unpleasant in the expression of his thoughts, he is able to de-escalate with each statement, seeing that his wife is not fighting back but is actually letting him have his say. At an appropriate time, when both are calm, they will have a discussion about this problem. At that point, the wife will explain her position, and they will negotiate toward a comfortable solution for them both. The wife will reap the benefits of her positive judgment and patience in terms of a positive solution and increased *shalom bayis*.

In the second example, we see how a wife's negative interpretation of her husband's words leads her to respond in a disrespectful and unpleasant manner. The "right" wife assumes that her husband is simply making a mistake in his wording without intending to hurt her. However, she does inform him that this wording can be hurtful even unintentionally and asks him to refrain from using it in the future. Her neutral judgment of his motives enables her to express herself pleasantly and calmly even while delivering a rebuke. If she wants to increase marital happiness, a wife should always opt for the most positive interpretation of her husband's behavior.

In the next chapters, we will encounter more strategies pertaining to negotiating and resolving differences. Although they may also pertain to the maintenance of a respectful relationship, their main characteristic lies in another domain— e.g., in the building of trust, affection, or intimacy.

The techniques that have been explored so far are pertinent to establishing the base-line of respect so essential in any marriage. When husband and wife treat each other with respect at all times, they create the environment in which love can flourish.

CHAPTER THREE
Building Trust

Trust is that characteristic of marriage which provides the union with emotional security. Both partners know that their marriage is "forever" and that they formed a true, inseparable family union when they merged under the *chupah*. Their allegiance is to each other before all others in the spirit of "Therefore a man shall leave his father and his mother and cleave to his wife, and they shall become one flesh."[1] This trust fortifies them through times of stress and marital challenge, permitting them to negotiate difficulties in a framework of permanence and good faith. Furthermore, trust enables husband and wife to interpret each other's behavior in the most positive light and contributes significantly to marital harmony.

Like respect, trust is a prerequisite to the formation of affection and intimacy in marriage. If a woman does not trust her
husband, she will not allow herself to become close to him.
Her suspicions will prevent her from loving him since her focus
on fear and negativity will not leave her open to such positive
feelings. Similarly, a man must trust his wife before he can
truly love her. Thus, it is essential that a wife utilize trust-building strategies in order to permit the growth of warm, loving
feelings in her marriage. Her efforts in this regard will ensure
that her husband will be able to trust her and he will, hopefully, respond with trustworthy behaviors on his part. If for some
reason he does not, marital counseling may be in order.

Trust is conveyed in many ways. When you show your
spouse that you are reliable and dependable, he knows he can
trust you. When you refrain from hurting him physically or
emotionally, he feels safe with you. When you establish an attitude of firm commitment to the marriage, he doesn't live with
fears of desertion. When you consistently give him the benefit
of the doubt, he breathes freely in his own home, knowing that
he can reach his potential in the environment created by his
wife. This chapter will explore the specific trust-building techniques which you can utilize to establish a secure basis of trust
in your relationship.

Techniques

19. Limit Your Friendly Dealings with Men

Your husband should feel totally confident of his place in
your life. He should not have to worry that you don't find him
sufficiently attractive or that you might be looking for more
male attention. Thus, you should endeavor to make him feel

that he is the only man in the world. After all, for you he IS the only man in the world! (And you are the only woman in the world for him, of course!)

A few basic rules help to convey this impression of singular importance:

Don't stare at other men.

Don't become involved in lengthy conversations with them.

Don't act in an overly casual or frivolous manner with them.

Don't become involved in helping anyone without your husband's express consent and acknowledgment.

Don't discuss previous men in your life (like the one you almost married).

Don't dress in a way which draws undue attention to yourself, even if it is within the technical bounds of halachah.

Do give your husband as much time and attention as you can reasonably manage.

Do make yourself attractive for him.

Of course, be careful to follow all of the halachos of *yichud*.[2]

These rules are not just for "Chassidishe" ladies. They are basic guidelines that all women should follow in order to earn the trust of their mates. Husbands are as prone to insecurity as their wives are; these safeguards prevent imaginations from running in destructive courses.

The basic message that a wife should ideally send to her husband is that he is the most important person in the world. Even if she pursues female friendships or outside activities to an excessive degree, she delivers a very different message: "Other people (things, activities) are more important to me than you are." Trust can be eroded when a wife demonstrates that the marriage is nearer the bottom of her list of priorities than the top. Her husband feels that he comes second or third or maybe even last in her life. This is a dangerous situation.

This is not to say that a woman should isolate herself in her home, speaking to no one other than her husband and doing nothing outside of her domestic responsibilities. It is only to caution her to divide her energies in a way which clearly states that her husband is her first priority. This accomplished, she is certainly free to have friends, interests, and commitments outside of her marital relationship. (Needless to say, a husband must also strive to make his wife his first priority.)

Example 1

wrong:

> husband: "Malky, I think you gave our Shabbos guest a bit too much attention today."

> wife: "Don't be ridiculous. I was only being friendly to him—after all, I was the hostess, and he was a guest in our home. Should I have been rude to him and ignored him?"

right:

> husband: "Malky, I think you gave our Shabbos guest a bit too much attention today."

> wife: "Oh. I didn't mean to give that impression at all. I thought I should act in a friendly manner towards him, but I certainly didn't think I was going overboard. Can you tell me exactly what I did that was 'too much'? I'll be careful to avoid those behaviors next time we have a guest."

Example 2

wrong:

>*husband:* "Do you think you could cut down on some of your community activities? You're always on the phone; I can never reach you when I call during the day. You're out every evening. The kids never see you. It's too much already."

>*wife:* "Don't be ridiculous. You're never home yourself! You want me to be here all of a sudden? If I can help the community, I think I should be doing it. The children aren't complaining, so why should you?"

right:

>*husband:* "Do you think you could cut down on some of your community activities? You're always on the phone; I can never reach you when I call during the day. You're out every evening. The kids never see you. It's too much already."

>*wife:* "If you think it's too much, Heshy, then I'll certainly cut down. Although I do enjoy my community work, I'm sure I could arrange to be a bit more available. Why don't you help me work out a revised schedule that meets your needs better?"

Comment:

In the first example, the "wrong" wife discounts her husband's feelings and concerns. She makes it appear as if he is being unreasonable in his perceptions. If this conversation does not develop into a full-blown argument, it will, at the minimum, ensure that husband and wife experience a degree of emotional separation. They will not have reached an "understanding" in the matter, resulting in a loss of trust on the husband's part.

The "right" wife spends less energy on defending and explaining herself and more energy on indicating that she is willing to please her husband. Her response shows that she takes
his complaint seriously. She is interested in making sure that
her husband feels secure and comfortable. Rather than challenge his insecurity, she indicates that she will do whatever is
necessary to foster the growth of trust.

Similarly, in the second example, the "wrong" wife discounts her husband's jealousy over her activities. Since she
thinks he's being irrational, she makes no effort to please him.
Her behavior will detract from marital trust and harmony. The
"right" wife attempts to compromise with her husband. Even
though she may also feel that her husband's feelings are unjus-
tified, she acknowledges that these are his feelings. She's not
about to give up all of her community work in order to ap-
pease him, but she is willing to make herself more available to
him so that he will feel that he is also important to her. Since
insecurity is, by definition, an irrational emotion, it is useless to
try to talk a person out of it. If it is severe, then individual
psychological counseling may be in order. If it is the normal insecurity that people experience periodically, then secure-
making behaviors are the cure. If a wife can help her husband
to trust her more by behaving in ways which build trust, then
she should try to do so. Ignoring or discounting trust problems
increases them rather than decreases them.

20. Live Up to Your Commitments

A commitment is basically a promise. When a wife
promises to take the children out for an hour so her husband
can get some work done in the house, she is obligated to carry

through. Failure to take the children out would constitute breaking her promise—which is the same as breaking her word or lying. We are halachically forbidden to deceive our fellow men and are obligated to speak truthfully.[3] We should be careful to make only those promises that we are prepared to keep. A wife who has trouble living up to her commitments impairs the growth of trust in her marital relationship. When a husband feels that he cannot rely on the word of his wife, he responds by not believing her promises. If he has seen too many occasions on which she said she would pay a specific bill and then failed to do so, said she would invite a guest and then "forgot," or said she would pick up some item for him at the store and then did not do it—then he gives up believing her. He can't trust her.

The use of vague language contributes to lack of communication which may result in the erosion of trust. Words like "maybe," "I'll try," and "we'll see" can all lead to serious disappointment. A husband may ask his wife if she can make fish for Shabbos. She responds, "I'll try." He imagines that this means she will most likely do it, whereas she actually means that there's little chance. In any event, when Shabbos comes and the fish doesn't, the husband's disappointment shades on anger. Didn't his wife indicate that she would try to make fish? Naturally, an unpleasant argument could easily ensue as the wife insists that she didn't make any promises and the husband insists that he was looking forward to this dish.

The more specific and realistic a wife is in her communication, the less danger there is of failing to live up to her commitments. If her husband invites her to go on a family outing on a Sunday afternoon, she should be specific about when she would like to go. For example, she might say, "I'd love to go after I give the children lunch. That would be around noon hour. Then it'll take me another twenty minutes to clean up and I'll be ready to go." If she had said, "I'd love to go after I give the children lunch," her husband might expect her to be ready as soon as everyone had finished eating. Not counting on the extra twenty minute wait, it appears to him that his wife is unreliable in her commitment. As much clarity and specificity as possible prevents this sort of problem. In fact, making reference to exact times on the clock ("I'll be ready at 12:40") and dates on the calendar ("I'll have it done by January 3rd") increases the accuracy and reliability of your communication. There is less opportunity for eroding trust.

Example 1

wrong:

> husband: "Will you be able to mend my blue pants for me this week?"
>
> wife: "Probably."

right:

> husband: "Will you be able to mend my blue pants for me this week?"
>
> wife: "I think so, but I don't know for sure right now. If it's really important to you, I'll make certain to find the time. Does it matter to you whether I get it done this week or next?"

Example 2

wrong:

> husband: "Didn't you say you were going to pick up the photographs today?"
>
> wife: "Yes, but it turned out I didn't have time."

husband: *"If you would have let me know you weren't going to do it, I could have done it. I was right near the store this afternoon."*

wife: *"Well, I'll get them tomorrow. Don't worry about it."*

husband: *"Yes, but I wanted them for tonight specifically. My brother is coming, don't forget, and he wanted a set to take back home. Now he won't be able to have one."*

wife: *"I'm sorry, but I can't always do these errands. I have a house full of children and things don't always work out for me to get out before the stores close."*

husband: *"Then don't tell me you're going to do it next time. I was counting on you."*

right:

husband: *"Didn't you say you were going to pick up the photographs today?"*

wife: *"Oh, I'm so sorry, Dovid! I should have told you earlier that it looked like I wasn't going to make it. I really thought I was going to be right by the store anyway, and that's why I offered to pick them up. Please forgive me. I know it was important."*

Comment:

In the first example, the "wrong" wife's vague reply invites misinterpretation. Her husband may need the pants and be relying on her to have them ready based on her answer. He will lose trust in her if she does not have them prepared.

The "right" wife attempts to clarify how essential it is to her husband that the pants be ready that week. If it is not urgent, she may not have them ready until the following week. However, if he explains that it is very important, then she will put aside other tasks and make sure that she has them ready for him. As a good communicator, she helps her spouse to be specific in his request. Her questions pinpoint his exact needs. She does not reply in a vague manner, nor does she accept a vague query. This ensures that lack of communication will not contribute to a buildup of mistrust.

We see in the second example how broken promises can lead to painful interactions between husband and wife. The "wrong" dialogue illustrates that it is better not to make promises than to make them casually. This wife is not even apologetic about her error, which adds insult to injury. Instead, she attempts to explain that it is unreasonable of her husband to expect a busy housewife like her to keep her word! At least in the "right" dialogue, the wife apologizes profusely for her mistake in making a promise that she couldn't keep. If a wife's working conditions do make it difficult for her to keep certain kinds of appointments or fulfill certain kinds of obligations, then she should be most careful not to commit herself to these things. In this way, although she may not always be able to help her husband when she would like to, she will at least contribute to the development and maintenance of basic trust in her marital relationship.

21. Keep Your Marriage Matters Private

Marriage partners must be able to trust each other with the private details of their lives. No husband should have to worry about his wife telling people about his personal behaviors and shortcomings. He should also feel confident that his private conversations with her in the home will remain private and not be shared with her friends or relatives. Should she complain to her mother or sister about her husband's speech or actions, she may be guilty of speaking *lashon hora*. In addition to committing this transgression, she erodes marital trust. Once her husband feels that others know about his private life, he will feel that he no longer has a private life. This causes enormous resentment.

Sometimes a distraught wife turns to many people to seek advice regarding a marital issue. She may consult with her parents, other relatives, and several friends. Each one has something to offer, and each one permits her to air her aggravations. However, each of these people is biased since they are all emotionally connected to the wife in some significant way. Each one is a lay person—not a professional counselor. Thus, each will offer amateur advice, not necessarily in the true interests of the wife. Some such "advisors" actually help people along to the divorce courts through improper suggestions. Some divorced friends are particularly poor advisors because they actively encourage a person to pursue their "rights" rather than marital happiness. (They may actually be eager to have another newly-single friend to join them.) Furthermore, too many pieces of advice can lead to increased confusion and distract one from effective problem solving. Finally, all of these "advisors" will develop negative feelings toward the husband as a result of hearing unpleasant things about him. Later, when husband and wife have managed to reconcile their differences, these people may remain unable to forgive him. They may never actually accept or really like him again. The wife will surely experience this coldness on the part of her friends and relatives, and it can detract from her marital stability.

Interestingly, there is really very little need for so much discussion about marriage problems. In many cases, a wife can analyze a problem herself and decide what needs to be done about it. Taking time for solitude and serious reflection can be of greater importance than running around looking for advice from others. In cases where her emotional tension is high and she needs to release it or "burst," then she can confide in one trusted advisor—be it her Rav, her *mashpiah*, a professional counselor, or a very carefully selected friend. (She should try her best to avoid a relative because of the lack of impartiality and problems of forgiving later on.) Confiding in one person is not the same as letting "the whole world" know about a marriage problem. However, even this should be done as rarely as possible. The wife should always attempt to work with her spouse directly in order to restore harmony. Only when she is at a total loss as to how to do this should she consult with another.

Example 1

wrong:

> *friend: "How does your husband like the* shul *here?"*
>
> *wife: "Actually, he thinks it needs better management."*

right:

> *friend: "How does your husband like the* shul *here?"*
>
> *wife: "If you want my husband's opinion, you'd better check with him."*

Example 2

wrong:

> *friend: "Aren't men something? They're always too busy to help out with housework, but if you invite them to sit down with you for a donut and coffee–that they have time for!"*

wife: "I know what you mean. Just yesterday my Noach told me he had no time to mow the lawn, and then the children managed to get him to take them out for ice cream!"

right:

friend: "Aren't men something? They're always too busy to help out with housework, but if you invite them to sit down with you for a donut and coffee–that they have time for!"

wife: "I guess we're no different. I'd certainly find time for a coffee-break if I was invited for one, wouldn't you? Speaking of which, why don't I put the kettle on for us? I've got some delicious cookies you must try!"

Comment:

In the first example, the wife speaks on behalf of her husband. This practice can destroy trust because a spouse may not want his private opinions stated in public. Indeed, the wife may be making such a statement to someone whom the husband particularly would not want to hear it. Since she has no way of knowing whether he himself would share his personal opinion with this person, she is safer not offering it. In showing respect for her husband's individuality and for his trust in her confidentiality, she should make a general rule not to make statements in his name. In any event, we are to treat all private conversations we have with a person as confidential, unless they are expressly declared as "repeatable."[4] Since a wife learns her husband's ideas and beliefs from her private conversations with him, she is not free to repeat them to others without his express permission.

In the "right" dialogue, the wife correctly directs her listener to her husband. If the person would like the husband's opinion, he should seek it from the husband directly. The wife can only speak for herself. In this way she preserves the privacy of her relationship and maintains the total trust of her husband.

The second example presents the common "invitation to speak *lashon hora.*" A friend obviously wants to spend a few minutes criticizing husbands. The "wrong" wife falls into the trap and relates a private incident about her husband which is complete *lashon hora.* The "right" wife refuses to accept the invitation to talk about her husband's foibles and redirects the conversation away from talebearing. If this friend is put off by this maneuver, then she is probably not a friend worth keeping. A wife's efforts to build marital trust occur in the absence as well as in the presence of her spouse. If everyone knows her as a person who avoids talking about others, then her husband, too, will feel completely safe with her, knowing that she isn't likely to be talking about him. This is a nice feeling for him to enjoy. On the other hand, a wife who likes to talk about people to her friends and to her husband erodes marital trust. Her husband will know that she is capable of speaking about him as well.

22. Allow Your Husband to Grow and Change

Since it is the task of every Jew to continuously strive for higher levels of personal development, it is important for husband and wife to support each other in this work. A wife should encourage her husband in his efforts to overcome his weaknesses and to build on his strengths. She must allow him to change and grow, forgiving his past mistakes and demonstrating faith in his potential for improvement. This she cannot do if she refuses to forget his past "offenses."

Forgetting is directly related to forgiving. When a wife sincerely forgives her husband for some wrong that he committed against her, she wipes it from her slate and recalls it no more. This, in fact, is how we are obligated to forgive others for wronging us.[5] Moreover, as we forgive others, so *Hashem* forgives us for our wrongs.[6] When we ask *Hashem* for forgiveness on Yom Kippur, we must do so with a pure heart, one that has generously forgiven those around us. If we follow the practice of forgiving others each night before retiring, we actively reduce the chances that we will hold a grudge against another person.[7] This is the best way to develop the skill of forgiving and forgetting.

A wife can help herself to "let go" of her grievances against her husband if she establishes a deadline for expressing them. For example, if her husband was late in meeting her at a designated location and his lateness greatly inconvenienced or distressed her, she might allow herself to refer to this incident for a maximum period of one month. Of course, it is preferable that she deal with the issue at once and completely resolve it, forgiving her husband totally. However, since her deadline is one month, she would be permitted to refer to this incident anytime during the one-month period if it seemed necessary. After that time, however, she is never permitted to refer to it again. It is as if it never happened. Just as *Hashem* forgives us totally on Yom Kippur, we forgive our spouse totally at the end of our "deadline" period. The sin is no longer recorded in our "books." By not mentioning the mistake again, the wife fulfills the halachah forbidding her to remind a person of his past misdeeds.[8]

This process of forgiveness prevents a wife from holding her spouse back by "pigeon-holing" him. Instead of labeling him as "a person who is late," she confronts individual issues and permits her image of her husband to remain flexible. She sees him as capable of changing. One mistake does not classify him as a person incapable of performance—it is viewed as only one mistake. Forgiveness permits the husband to overcome negative patterns. Just as *Hashem* continuously waits for all of us to overcome our faults, a wife can patiently wait for her husband to conquer his shortcomings. As long as he lives, the potential exists that he will improve.

Example 1

wrong:

> *husband: "I think I'll fix the garage door this Sunday."*
>
> *wife: "Sure, sure."*
>
> *husband: "What does that mean?"*
>
> *wife: "It means that you probably won't fix the garage door this Sunday just like you didn't fix it last Sunday, and just like you didn't fix the kids' bikes last month, and just like you never find time to fix anything around here."*

right:

> *husband: "I think I'll fix the garage door this Sunday."*
>
> *wife: "Great! I'd really appreciate that because it's so hard for me to open every day. I'm so pleased you're going to take care of it."*

Example 2

wrong:

> *husband: "Do you mind if I borrow your good scissors for a few minutes?"*
>
> *wife: "Yes, I do mind. Last time you took them you kept them*

*in your drawer for a month afterward and I couldn't find them
when I needed them."*

husband: *"Leah, that was two years ago!"*

right:

husband: *"Do you mind if I borrow your good scissors for a
few minutes?"*

wife: *"Go ahead, Levy, but please put them back in my sewing
drawer right away."*

Comment:

In the "wrong" dialogue of the first example, the wife is
responding to her unpleasant experience of being constantly
let down by her husband. He is forever promising to do things
that he doesn't carry through. Through bitter experience, the
wife has come to expect that he cannot be relied upon to do
repairs around the house. This disappointment leads to her
sarcastic "sure, sure" response and her tirade about his poor
track record. However, both of these replies are
counterproductive. He sees that she expects him to fail to
keep his word. He realizes that she views him as unable or un-
willing to do repair work. Accordingly, he will "live down" to
her expectations: what's the use of trying when no one expects you to succeed anyway?

In the "right" dialogue, the wife perseveres in her optimism
that her husband can make changes. Despite her previous dis-
appointments, she shows him that she believes him and trusts
him. Her enthusiasm for his project encourages him. With her
support, he might just overcome his natural tendencies this
time. As he sees that she expects him to succeed, he is
motivated to live up to her expectations.

Even if the husband should let his wife down one more time, her response to his announcement was valuable in itself. After all, a sarcastic or hostile response can only lead to arguments and ill feelings. A positive and encouraging reply keeps the mood pleasant and thus contributes to *shalom bayis*. The wife's refusal to refer back to previous failings permits her husband to move forward whenever he is ready to do so. She thus optimizes his potential for growth, which is one of her functions as an *aizer k'negdo*. Hopefully he will reward her efforts one day by making the desired changes.

Example two illustrates the wrong and right ways to handle one's memory of past misdeeds. In the "wrong" dialogue, the wife reminds her husband of a mistake he made two years ago and she acts as if it were made that morning. The "right" wife also remembers the problem she had with his borrowing scissors in the past, but she gives him permission to borrow them now because she has forgiven this past crime. Since it is important to her that she has them available, she does remind him to place them in the proper location after use. She does not, however, refer to the fact that one time, long ago, he didn't do this! In this way, she permits her husband to act differently in the present than he did in the past and demonstrates the trust she has in him.

23. Create Emotional Safety

Trust in marriage implies total emotional safety: one can rely on one's spouse to be straightforward, reasonable, predictable, honest, and kind. A husband cannot trust a wife who is erratic and unpredictable in her behavior, who is sometimes calm and other times highly excitable, sometimes kind and other times cruel. He needs to know that he is safe from emotional abuse.

The normal course of daily interactions does not generally provide a threat to emotional stability. Rather, it is during moments of conflict that the potential exists for destructive outbursts. In the heat of anger and frustration, a person may lose control. Thus, a wife may, in her frustration and exasperation, threaten to leave her husband or insist on a divorce. In the midst of the argument, she demands that he call a Rav to arrange a *get*. Perhaps she wonders aloud why she ever married him, claiming that this was a major mistake on her part. There are even women whose level of desperation leads them to threaten suicide. Naturally such threats and statements hurt to the core (which they are designed to do). They place the marriage on a thin line, stretched close to the breaking point. Once the suggestion is made that the marriage is something which can or should be terminated, the foundation of trust is destroyed. From that point on, one never knows where he stands and is constantly afraid that the fragile union may collapse. No marriage can tolerate the threat of divorce; love cannot grow in the absence of complete trust. Even if the marriage should last, it will not be characterized by the relaxed happiness that makes life worth living together.

There are other, less drastic means of destroying trust in marriage. Any form of emotional desertion has this consequence. Thus, if during an angry episode, a wife walks out of the house, locks herself in her room behind a slammed door, insists that her husband leave the premises immediately, or refuses to have contact with him in any way, she conveys a message of desertion. Her behavior states clearly that she is temporarily leaving him. Even prolonged sulking has this effect. For example, after an argument some women "punish" their husbands by not talking to them for several hours or even days. All of these ways of pushing oneself away from one's spouse cause severe strain on the relationship. They all interfere with emotional safety because they imply the possibility of permanent desertion.

All of this damage results from carelessness in speech. When people learn how to control their temper, they will control their speech and refrain from saying or doing those things which cause irreparable harm to their relationships. The Torah teaches us that one who has a bad temper destroys his own life, since anger will ruin his relationships with people and destroy his health and happiness. Moreover, his anger leads him to many aveiros.[9] As a primary example, in our anger we are likely to transgress the halachah which forbids us to use words which will cause anguish to others.[10] Obviously, threatening to leave one's husband must cause extreme anguish. This and other similar threats of desertion have two purposes behind them: 1) to inflict pain on one's marital partner and 2) to express one's utter despair. Although we are not expected to be angels, the Torah does not condone the infliction of emotional pain, even in retaliation for pain inflicted on oneself (and in fact, highly lauds those who refuse to retaliate in the face of insult and injury).[11] Secondly, one's despair can be expressed in ways which do not harm the fabric of one's marriage. Therefore, there is no reason to resort to this destructive technique, and much reason to refrain from using it.

Example 1

wrong:

> *husband:* "I'm fed up with your complaints!"

> *wife:* "Fine. So call your lawyer and let's get a divorce already!"

right:

> *husband:* "I'm fed up with your complaints!"

> *wife:* "Well, I'm pretty unhappy too. I hate these arguments we keep having! I want us to do something about it already. I'm too upset to discuss it now, but tomorrow we'd better sit down and figure out what we're going to do."

Example 2

wrong:

> *husband:* "Look, if you can't talk about this reasonably, I don't want to discuss it anymore."

> *wife:* "Fine. You hate me. I know, you just can't stand the sight of me. I don't even know why you married me in the first place."

Comment:

In the first example, the husband's provocative statement is the climax of a heated argument. Obviously, he himself is not using appropriate communication strategies. In the "wrong" example, the wife responds in like fashion to his tirade and makes her own inappropriate response. She implies that the marriage should be terminated if he is so unhappy. Such a statement plants the first seeds of instability and uncertainty in their union. Unfortunately, once words are spoken, they cannot be retrieved. The psychological and spiritual damage is done.

The "right" wife manages to express her unhappiness without escalating. Her statement makes it clear that she does not want things to go on as they are, but does not suggest that the solution is dissolution of the marriage! On the contrary, she invites her husband to work with her toward an improved way of relating. This demonstrates her optimism and commitment to the permanency of the marriage, thus contributing strongly to the growth of emotional safety.

In the second example, the wife acts irrationally by pretending that her husband said something that he didn't say at all. He only said that he didn't want to continue the discussion. She then made it seem as if he had said that he hated her and didn't want to be married to her. She put extremely destructive words into his mouth. By acting as if these were his true intentions, she becomes as angry at him as if he had actually said these things. This kind of communication is extremely harmful to the emotional stability of a couple because it is so irrational. Crazy communications destroy trust in marriage.

The anger and bitterness of these kinds of conversations generally occur when a couple discusses a particularly sensitive subject. For some couples, all too many subjects are "particularly sensitive" (and such people may benefit from counseling), but for most, there are only a couple of such volatile issues within their relationship. Although common troublesome issues are finances, household responsibilities, and in-laws, each couple may have its unique areas of concern. If you identify such an area affecting your marriage, adhering to the following strategies can prevent the build-up of rage and frustration leading to the use of highly destructive communication strategies:

a) Do not discuss your difficult issues spontaneously. Always schedule a time for them. If one seems to arise on the "spur of the moment," refrain from pursuing it then and diplomatically urge your husband to postpone the conversation until a mutually convenient moment. A standard format for making this arrangement is to issue an invitation to meet at such-and-such a time to have a brief talk about such-and-such an issue, to be followed by a certain pleasurable experience: e.g., "Yitzchak, could we meet at 9:00 tonight for five minutes to discuss our upcoming visit to your mother's house? Afterwards we can have a delicious danish and coffee." It is extremely important to put a maximum time limit on these stressful conversations. DO NOT GO BEYOND THE LIMIT EVEN IF YOU HAVEN'T FINISHED DISCUSSING THE ISSUE. You can make another appointment to finish the conversation another day. The first time you meet for a sensitive issue, set the maximum at five or ten minutes. For subsequent meetings on the same issue, you can gradually extend the time to fifteen minutes. Never discuss a sensitive issue for more than twenty minutes at one time. Always follow a discussion of painful issues with a lovely positive interlude—use your imagination! Some common "rewards" for successfully completing a discussion without becoming hostile are: food and beverage treats, a brief outing, exchange of small gifts, enjoying a relaxing activity together, or working on some pleasant and/or amusing project like your picture album. Whatever you choose should be something that will make both of you feel happy and close. Try to do something, no matter how small, to reinforce your progress (if nothing else, you can always smile and say "well done!").

b) If the discussion should start to get unpleasant, stop it promptly. Do so before you get very angry. Still speaking calmly and pleasantly, you can say, "I'm beginning to feel a little uncomfortable. I'd rather continue the conversation tomorrow night before things deteriorate. If we stop now, we can still enjoy our little 'reward' for discussing this without hurting each other." Always be sure to keep the appointments you make. Failure to do so can lead to a serious breakdown of trust.

c) If you simply cannot discuss certain issues without engaging in destructive communication, arrange to meet with a third party (Rav or trusted counselor) to help you do so. There is no need to wait until you are desperately unhappy to do this—prevention of irreparable marital damage is a priority. Once pain has been inflicted, it is very difficult to restore the trust and emotional safety required in marriage.

24. Remain Adult

Trust occurs in a relationship in which two adults can communicate with each other. They trust each other to respond in rational and logical ways. They trust each other with their possessions and bodies. This sort of trust cannot exist when a marriage partner regresses emotionally.

Regression refers to the state in which a full-grown adult acts like a very young child. When an adult woman acts as helpless as a preschooler, she is regressing. When she has a temper-tantrum like a toddler, she is regressing. When she bursts into tears, she is regressing. All of these forms of regression lead to emotional desertion—you cannot have a grown-up relationship with a two-year-old. When a woman refuses to act in a grown-up manner, she leaves her husband emotionally alone.

Helpless behaviors include the inability to make decisions, refusal to accept responsibility, and refusal to act independently. Although a husband is "master" of his house in a Torah home, this position refers to his dominance in the spiritual realm.[12] In fact, a Jewish woman is the leader in matters regarding the home[13] and, according to some opinions, in all worldly matters as well.[14] Certainly a Jewish woman is not considered to be a child who cannot think or act independently. On the contrary, she has mature obligations to *Hashem* from the time she is bas mitzvah and is not exempt from acting in a responsible, adult fashion from that point on. Passivity, incompetence, and other "helpless" behaviors are used to set up a situation in which a wife can "blame" her husband for things that go wrong. For example, a wife who claims that she's not good at cooking can insist that her husband prepare the Shabbos meals. This relieves her of a task and also provides an opportunity for her to complain to him about how and when he does this job! A wife who plays helpless may blame her husband for being insensitive or unkind when she herself has not taken strong steps to work with him toward improved communication. A "helpless" player may accuse her husband of spoiling the children when she does nothing constructive to stop the situation. If a wife uses anything less than her full adult capabilities in her marriage, she robs her husband of a full mate and invites trust-threatening interactions.

Throwing a tantrum is another childlike behavior that some people engage in. It includes screaming and yelling, throwing and hitting, stomping and slamming. Toddlers use tantrums to express their utter exasperation and anger because they do not yet have sufficient verbal skills with which to express themselves. Moreover, they lack the emotional maturity and control of older people. This causes them to escalate—to exaggerate the awfulness of the moment. A husband should be able to feel confident that he is dealing with a rational adult, even during times of disagreement and confrontation. After all, such times are unavoidable in marriage. If a wife begins to have a tantrum when things don't go her way, he loses trust in her. How can he relate to a raging child? This sort of anger is the type that our Sages describe as akin to idol worship, in which the angry person will commit all sorts of transgressions as he lets his emotions overrule him.[15]

Finally, a woman may regress by dissolving into tears. It is well recognized that women are brought more easily to tears than are men. The Gemara states: "A man must always be careful not to hurt his wife, for since her tears are quick to come, she is easily hurt."[16] Thus a woman's emotionality may in fact lead her to be saddened more readily than a man. Nonetheless, women must be careful not to USE this sensitivity as an opportunity to escape from adult negotiations. A husband cannot trust a wife who "disappears" into her tears when he wants to communicate with her. Tears are appropriate for true moments of grief and actual pain, but they are inappropriate when used to halt communication, as if to say, "You are hurting me too much. I don't want to talk about this anymore." If a wife is truly hurt by her husband's cruel statements she might cry. However, if she chooses to do so, she should also state, "I'm too upset to talk about this right now. Let's meet in an hour when I'm calm enough to deal with this issue." In this manner she indicates that she is basically available for important negotiations. She is not using her tears as a weapon to silence her husband in the midst of unpleasant confrontations.

Example 1

wrong:

> husband: "Let's talk about this credit card account. We need to get control of the situation."
>
> wife: "Oh, you know I don't know anything about the accounts. Couldn't you just take care of it yourself?"

right:

> husband: "Let's talk about this credit card account. We need to get control of the situation."
>
> wife: "All right. I think we should pick a quiet time when the kids are sleeping so I can concentrate. You know I find this sort of thing difficult."

Example 2

wrong:

> wife: "You've got to stay home and help me get ready for Pesach. I just can't do this alone."
>
> husband: "I would if I could, Brachah, but I can't take more time off from work. I'm taking off Chol HaMoed as it is."
>
> wife: "It's too bad. Just tell them you can't make it. I'll go crazy otherwise. I can't cope with the house, the kids, and Pesach all by myself. You've got to take off at least a week to help me.
>
> husband: "Brachah, be reasonable. Other women manage somehow. Why can't you? I'll help as much as I can in the evenings and on Sundays. Maybe you're trying to do too much. Let's just do the minimum that is halachically required so you won't overstrain yourself."
>
> wife: "No! I need you here and that's it! Maybe other women can do it, but I can't. I just can't take the pressure! You've got to take at least three or four days off to help me."

right:

> wife: "You've got to stay home and help me get ready for Pesach. I just can't do it alone."

> husband: "I would if I could, Brachah, but I can't take off more time from work. I'm taking off Chol HaMoed as it is."

> wife: "O.K. If you can't help me, then let's hire help. I feel I can't manage it by myself."

> husband: "That could get expensive. Maybe you could just do less preparation."

> wife: "No, even the minimum takes everything out of me. I've got to have help–either you or someone else. Another solution is to pack up and go visit someone for Pesach. Maybe you've got some other ideas worth mentioning."

> husband: "If it's really important to you, I guess we'll just have to find some solution. Let's talk about it some more when I get home tonight."

Comment:

In the first example, when the wife claims that the task is too difficult for her, she places the burden solely upon her husband. He must then, like a father rather than a husband, solve the problem alone. At such times, a husband feels that he cannot rely upon his wife for adult companionship and so loses an element of trust in her.

When the wife agrees to work together with her husband on this mutual problem, he feels that he can trust her to be with him in stressful times as well as good times. She lets him know that this task is difficult for her, but she does not attempt to escape from it in a guise of helplessness. Indeed, she forces herself to confront the difficulty and thus grows in her own competence even as she assists her husband. She functions as a true *aizer k'negdo*, pushing herself beyond her limitations in order to be of assistance to her husband.

In the second example, the wife also acts like a helpless child in the "wrong" dialogue. Although her problem may be valid (perhaps she is physically weak due to a recent illness or birth), her approach is unreasonable. Her husband has mature commitments to his place of occupation. He can't just get up and leave because his wife wants him to do so. There are other more pragmatic solutions to her problem which she begins to explore in the "right" dialogue. When she focuses on realistic problem-solving, she is remaining in her adult state. When she focuses on unrealistic solutions, however, she is regressing to a childish state. Such regression is destructive to the process of marital trust and negotiation.

25. Avoid Surprises

Surprises can be a pleasant aspect of life. When they are very small and relatively rare, they can be a positive means of showing affection. For example, a wife may surprise her husband by buying him his favorite chocolate bar for a treat. However, large surprises can have quite the opposite effect. Instead of increasing affection, they can erode basic trust. If a wife surprises her husband with a new dining room set that she purchased, he may be understandably distressed. When an item is expensive, it is not appropriate "surprise" material. ("Expensive" is a relative term, depending on the couple's financial situation. For example, although a husband may like to buy his wife jewelry, his wife may not appreciate it if she feels the cost takes away from more basic necessities that they need.) In fact, a couple might make a prearranged agreement that they will not individually purchase items costing more than a certain baseline figure without the consent of the other spouse. The amount of the baseline would depend on the financial situation of the couple. Generally speaking, nobody likes unexpected bills, so a wife would be wise to let her husband know about her expenditures even when they do fall under their baseline agreement. This would avoid the situation in which he opens the credit card bill and finds twenty-five "surprise" items on it.

Earning the trust of one's husband in the financial realm is important to every marriage, but there are many other categories of surprises that can also pose a threat to the establishment of trust. For example, a wife may be tempted to surprise her husband in the domestic realm as she tidies up his desk or den for him. She may want to neaten, straighten, and "prune" the papers she finds there. She is the one who is surprised when she finds that he is unpleasantly enraged instead of pleasantly surprised at her efforts! He wants his private things left as he arranged them and far from appreciates her attempts at reorganization. If your husband prefers that his belongings remain untouched, respect his wishes. Don't secretly throw out his garbage or straighten up his mess. It is better to live with his clutter than to threaten your marital happiness by eroding his trust in you.

Another kind of surprise you would do well to avoid is in the social realm: don't invite guests that you haven't told your husband about. A man likes to feel that his house is a territory that he controls. Although he may enjoy the mitzvah of *hachnosas orchim*, it is common courtesy to check with him about the *orchim* you are preparing to invite. This prevents a situation in which he finds himself with guests he is uncomfortable with. He comes to trust that you will not put him into awkward situations and that you will take his wishes into account.

Surprises have the potential to disappoint their recipients. Moreover, there are some people who don't enjoy anything which is unexpected (e.g., changing your plans for a particular outing). Even those who are more flexible may find themselves angry as a result of some surprise they do not appreciate (e.g., a husband who in unhappy about a type of wallpaper his wife chose for the hallway without consulting him). Certain surprises are inherently disrespectful of a person's needs for time or space (e.g., inviting twenty girls over for a sleep-over party for your daughter without checking with your husband). Since surprises may lead to angry interactions, they should be carefully limited.

Example 1

wrong:

> *husband:* "What time do you want dinner tonight, Chavah?"

> *wife:* "Oh, I didn't get around to making dinner today. I thought you could pick us up a pizza or something in an hour or so."

Example 2

wrong:

> *husband:* "What is THAT?"

> *wife:* "It's my new dress for the wedding tonight. Don't you like it?"

> *husband:* "Well, I don't want to hurt your feelings, Chavah, but I really don't think you should wear that out. The color is much too loud and the style is totally inappropriate. Who sold you that thing anyway?"

wife: "You can't be serious! This is my only dress! I bought it specifically for tonight. I thought you'd love it, and I was really looking forward to surprising you with it."

husband: "You certainly did surprise me with it alright! Next time, I think you better skip the surprise and show me your purchase when you still have time to exchange it."

Comment:

As we see in the first example, not giving someone advance notice also results in unpleasant "surprises." It could well be that the husband has something else on his schedule that evening and wouldn't have the time to pick up dinner. Even if he had the time, he might not have budgeted for that particular expense. It might also be that he was looking forward to a good homemade meal and now has to resign himself to something that he doesn't really want. Receiving short notice about these dinner plans could easily lead to ill feelings and arguments. On the other hand, of course, the husband may have no objection at all to going to pick up pizza. However, the wife has no way of knowing this without asking. In order to avoid the possibility of disappointment, irritation, or anger, she should ask him the question about dinner early enough in the day that she could easily alter her plans if necessary. For example, if she realizes by 2 p.m. that her own schedule will not permit her to make a meal, she should ask him around that time if he would be willing and able to purchase dinner later that day. This gives him an opportunity to be an equal partner in plans that concern him. He can organize his own schedule to accommodate the new arrangement. He also has time to adjust his expectations and to make alternate suggestions if he prefers. Perhaps he doesn't like the idea of pizza and would be perfectly willing to make the dinner himself. With advance notice, he would be able to plan his menu and buy the ingredients he needs. This would permit him to feel comfortable with a change in the regular routine and would prevent him from feeling the anger associated with an undesired surprise.

In the second example, we see the potentially disastrous effects of surprising one's husband with a new dress. Often husbands have strong feelings about the clothes their wives wear. When a wife purchases an important article of clothing, particularly one she will be wearing around her husband, she would do well to try it on for him as soon as she can. If he has any objection to it, she can then return her purchase and try again. Everyday clothing may not require such effort, but expensive or important articles are worth the investment of time to please one's spouse.

26. Be Consistent

Consistency is very important in the establishment of trust. We have already discussed one type of consistency in the section "Live Up to Your Commitments." There we pointed out the importance of being consistent in carrying out your promises. However, there are additional forms of consistency in human behavior.

Perhaps the most crucial type of consistency is that found between body language and verbal language. A husband can trust a wife who says she is angry and looks annoyed even as she speaks. He may not be happy to see this emotional expression, but at least he understands it. On the other hand, an angry looking wife who claims that she's not at all upset is an enigma. Her words contradict her body language. Even if her facial features are relaxed and calm, it could be that her voice is sullen or sulky. This, too, would suggest that some emotion is present, but her denial confuses the issue. Giving such "mixed messages" leads to definite problems in communication. Should the husband respond to the words or to the body? Which can he trust?

Mixed messages tend to be given when a person experiences some ambivalence or uncertainty. For example, a husband may ask his wife if she would have time to pick up his clothes at the cleaners. Her grumpy tone of voice as she replies in the positive likely suggests that part of her is willing and able to fulfill his wish while part of her resents the added burden in her already busy day. Nonetheless, it is unfair of her to communicate her divided feelings in a confusing manner. It would be much better for her to say something like, "I would love to get your clothes for you, but I have so many things planned for today already. Could it wait until later this week?" If for some reason the clothes must be gotten that day, she could say, "I'll get them for you today, but it means that I'll have to rush through some of my other obligations. That causes me stress which makes it hard for me to deal with the children. In the future, I would appreciate it if you would give me enough notice that I could select a convenient day for myself to go and fetch your things, and I could arrange my schedule to best accommodate the extra chore." Now her husband would know exactly what's on her mind and would be able to trust her communication.

A wife should be aware that her facial expression conveys a message all of its own. Suppose that it is Yom Tov. The table is beautifully set, the house is sparkling, and the family is dressed in their best clothes. The wife has prepared a delicious meal which she is now serving. However, after all of her Yom Tov preparations, she is understandably fatigued. At this particular meal they have no guests; she is functioning in her relaxed state as "herself." She serves dinner with a drawn, pained look on her face. This look erases the joy of Yom Tov. It completely dampens the mood of the occasion despite her invitation to everyone to "eat and enjoy." The look on her face speaks louder than her words, but the message is still inconsistent. On the one hand, her efforts say, "Let's make Yom Tov special and beautiful," but on the other hand, her facial features say, "Yom Tov is too hard and unpleasant." Her entire family will receive both messages, unfortunately, and none will be immune to the mistrust which results.

Consistency also involves taking one's own words seriously enough to remember them. A wife should be able to reliably remember what she said and what demands she made on her family members. It causes difficulties if a husband says, "Sarah, you said you wanted all the kids to go to camp this summer," and his wife responds, "I never said that! I said the older three should go." If this sort of conversation happens frequently, communicative trust is eroded. In other words, if a wife frequently denies that she said things, her husband cannot trust her when she makes a statement. He'll learn that she is all too likely to deny the statement later on. A wife must pay as much attention to her own speech as she hopes others will! She must only say that which she herself takes seriously. If she chatters without thinking, she may say many things that she doesn't actually mean. A Jew should always weigh his words to be sure that they will not cause harm to others.[17] Words spoken without commitment and sincerity certainly have the potential to cause pain later on.

Example 1

wrong:

> husband: "What's wrong?"
>
> wife (looking miserable): "Nothing."

right:

> husband: "What's wrong?"
>
> wife: "I'm depressed. I don't want to discuss it now. Ask me in a couple of hours."

Example 2

wrong:

> wife (banging the plate down on the table): "Here's your dinner."
>
> husband: "What are you so grumpy about?"
>
> wife: "I'm tired, you know! I was up all night with the baby, and I just don't have the energy to do everything. I'm too tired to serve everyone dinner on days like this."
>
> husband: "So why are you serving dinner? You could ask the children to do it or you could ask me, or we could just all help ourselves. I'd rather you sit down and relax than bang my food on the table. You're not doing yourself or anyone else a favor by serving us an angry dinner!"

Comment:

In the first example, when the wife denies that she's unhappy but obviously looks miserable, she causes her husband to mistrust her communication. However, when she tells him flatly that she's not happy at the moment, she establishes her reliability. It is most important that the husband show respect for his wife at this point. Since she says she's not up to discussing her problem just then, he must leave her until she feels she is ready. It is hard enough for a grumpy person to summon the consideration required to answer the question in the first place! She should not be pushed to explain further at that time.

In the second example, a wife gives two opposing messages simultaneously: I serve you dinner because I love to take care of you; and, I don't want to serve you dinner because I'm too exhausted right now. As her husband points out, the mixed message is received primarily as a negative message. Her anger and resentment overshadow her positive intentions. It would be better for everyone if she simply let them know that she couldn't serve (or make) dinner that night. No one appreciates a martyr—a person who looks miserable doing something that ought to convey love. Consistency in words and actions is the best route.

27. Be Accurate and Truthful

One cannot expect to develop trust in a marriage in which truth is taken casually. A wife must always distance herself from an untruth, as the Torah urges us.[18] Although most people refrain from complete lies (such as saying they were cleaning the house when they actually were shopping), many are less careful about exaggerations and embellishments. Thus, a wife might say that her husband kept her waiting for half an hour when it was actually closer to fifteen minutes. There is, in fact, no need for her to enlarge his offence since he should not keep her waiting at all if they have made an appointment. If she was inconvenienced or made uncomfortable by the delay, it is really irrelevant whether her discomfort was fifteen minutes more or less—what matters is that she was put out. In general, if a person has a valid complaint, it will stand on its own without exaggeration. If the point being made seems to require embellishment, it probably shouldn't be made at all. Moreover, as we learn from our Sages: "If you add to the truth, you subtract from it."[19] A perfectly reasonable complaint may not be heard at all as a husband concentrates on defending himself against the exaggerated point. For example, the husband in the above example may argue that he was not half an hour late, that the delay couldn't have been more than ten minutes or so. In focusing on this point, he will miss the essential point, which is that his wife was upset and inconvenienced by his lateness. Her exaggeration thus weakens her argument significantly.

Many "lies" start off rather innocently. For example, a husband might ask his wife what time she will be home from her shopping expedition. She says she will be back by 6 p.m. As it turns out, she's not home until 8:30. Of course she had no way of knowing that she would be delayed by long lines, traffic congestion, and a surprise sale. Nonetheless, if this sort of incident happens repeatedly, her husband will lose trust in her ability to tell the truth. Rather than commit oneself to an arrangement which contains many unknown variables (like the shopping expedition), it would be better to answer such a question by saying, "I hope to be back by 6 p.m., but if it looks like I'll be delayed, I'll call you around 5:45 to let you know." This answer is really more honest. Obviously the wife could have come back at 6 p.m. if she felt it was essential to do so.

She simply would have left her items at the cash register and left the store, leaving the long lines behind her. She would have ignored the surprise sale and plowed along home, knowing that she committed herself to being there by a certain time. In fact, this is exactly what she would have done if she had had an "important" appointment at that hour. Her actual behavior indicates that she really meant to say, "I'd like to be home around 6 p.m., but if anything detains me, I'll stay as long as necessary to finish my errands." She certainly didn't mean to lie when she told her husband what time she would return, yet she obviously did not consider her words as a serious commitment. This sort of miscommunication is harmless if it happens quite rarely, but destructive to the trust-building process if it occurs with regularity.

Other innocent lies take place when a wife feels obligated to provide information which she really doesn't possess. For example, her husband might ask her how much it will cost to have the rugs cleaned. She guesses that it will be under a hundred dollars. He then tells her to go ahead and get them done. The bill comes in at well over a hundred dollars, and the husband is quite upset. His wife points out that she herself was only guessing when she stated the original price, but he claims that he trusted her opinion and experience in the matter and was therefore relying on her guess when he told her to pursue the cleaning. This episode could have been easily avoided had the wife simply said, "I don't know how much it will cost. I'll call and get some estimates." Our Sages warn that a person should become accustomed to admitting, "I don't know" if he wants to avoid lying.[20] Again, if this kind of miscommunication happens regularly, the husband will eventually lose trust in his wife's word.

Another inadvertent, but trust-destroying, lie occurs when a wife promises to do something for her husband and then fails to carry through. This failure to live up to her commitment may not have been at all intentional, but is still considered wrong.[21] Repeated episodes of failure to carry through results in loss of trust.

Example

wrong:

> *wife: "Every time I ask you to do something for me you're too busy! You never help me out at all!"*

right:

> *wife: "I asked you to take out the garbage twice this week and you didn't do it. I had to do it myself. What can we do to avoid this happening in the future?"*

Comment:

In the "wrong" example, the wife uses the misleading words "every" and "never." These words (and others like "always" and "completely") are very rarely accurate descriptions. It is most likely that this husband complies with his wife's wishes at least "sometimes," and he will therefore tend to focus on her "lie" when responding to her remark. An argument will ensue concerning whether he NEVER helps out or whether he does do so once in a while. This argument will then miss the real issue, which is that the wife is feeling unhappy about some specific issue happening right now and needing resolution.

In the "right" example, the wife sticks to the honest facts when making her complaint. Instead of making generalizations (calling him names like inconsiderate, selfish, or lazy) or over-generalizations (saying that he never helps with the garbage), she simply states the most recent aspect of the problem, even if the problem has been on-going for some time. This invites him to become involved in realistic problem-solving rather than petty fighting over the accuracy of exaggerations. Oversimplifications are too close to untruths to be acceptable forms of communication. Staying accurate and truthful increases trust between marriage partners.

28. Respect Your Husband's Emotional Limits

Your intimate relationship with your husband gives you access to information few other people have about him. You alone know just what irritates him, what are his secret fears, and what are his insecurities. He trusts you not to abuse your privileged knowledge by using this information against him. Of course, a wife is not likely to do that unless she is in a state of rage and is purposefully attempting to hurt her husband. Thus, as we've said many times already, it is essential that we learn to control our anger.

What constitutes this sort of emotional abuse? Suppose a wife knows that her husband intensely dislikes his boss at work. During an argument, she might mention that her husband closely resembles that boss! She correctly anticipates that this will infuriate him. She incorrectly assumes that this minor victory can help her "win" her argument. In fact, she suffers a very serious loss as her husband withdraws from her and the trust between them is destroyed.

A wife may feel that her husband has an unreasonable reaction to something. Since it is, in her eyes, unreasonable, she insists on confronting him with it. For example, she knows that he has a fear of flying. Despite this knowledge, she books a flight for the two of them for their vacation, on the assumption that the only way he will get over his fear is if he faces it head on. When he reacts violently to her action, she feels like a poor martyr, badly treated by her irrational mate who she was only trying to help. However, the fault for this unpleasant episode is entirely her own. She knew in advance that her husband was sensitive in regard to the subject of flight. Her mistake was in ignoring his particular foibles. All people have unreasonable and irrational concerns or tastes. A wife must respect her husband's peculiarities and preferences if she wants to earn his trust. She should remember that she has no responsibility to educate him to overcome his fears, but has a great responsibility to foster *shalom bayis* by respecting his wishes and feelings.

Respecting a husband's emotional limits means that a wife will refrain from doing or saying that which she knows will upset him. Because of her intimate knowledge of him, she certainly has the power to hurt him severely. However, since her marital goal is happiness and peacefulness, she will always be careful not to hit in his weak spots. In fact, most marital arguments could be avoided altogether if each partner held himself or herself back from doing that which they knew upset their spouses. If a wife overspends, knowing her husband will be annoyed, she has provoked an argument. If she asks him repeatedly to do some chore when she knows he can't tolerate nagging, she has provoked an argument. If she insults him for not carrying out his responsibilities, knowing that this will hurt and anger him, she has provoked an argument. Yet it will be the wife who will suffer as a result of all of these disputes, just as much as her husband will. The feeling after all arguments is regret.[22] The wife knows that she is ruining her own marital happiness by not carefully respecting the emotional limits of her husband.

Example

wrong:

> husband: *"Isn't dinner ready yet?"*

> wife: *"I'm working as fast as I can, Levi. I'm not a short-order cook, you know. If you're so impatient, why don't you get in here and help out?"*

right:

> husband: *"Isn't dinner ready yet?"*

> wife: *"No."*

Comment:

In the "wrong" example, the wife responds defensively and angrily to her husband's impatience. If she would take the time to think before she opens her mouth, however, she would realize that what she is about to say will likely irritate him. She knows that he never helps in the kitchen, so her invitation to him to do so is highly sarcastic and bitter. Although the husband was in error himself when he phrased his request as he did, this does not excuse the wife from her own part in creating strife. Her responsibility (just like his) is to pursue peace in her home.[23] As an *aizer k'negdo*, she can rise above her husband's error, rather than sink down to his level. If she makes it a practice never to respond instantaneously to a provocation, but gives herself a couple of minutes to think about how her words will affect her husband, then she will be able to pursue the mitzvah of seeking peace. Obviously this will be hardest to do when she is unkindly provoked or when they are both in the middle of a disagreement, but the reward for controlling herself at such times is even greater.[24] Moreover, the Talmud states that when a person consciously decides not to cause pain to someone who has vexed him, he is forgiven for his transgressions.[25] Thus, in addition to the marital benefits she accrues from her restraint, she may receive great spiritual rewards for being considerate of her husband's feelings and emotional limitations.

29. Learn to Apologize

When a wife apologizes and asks forgiveness from her husband for causing him anguish, she takes an important step in establishing trust within the relationship. Her husband realizes that her intentions are good, that she regrets any pain that she causes, and that she intends to be careful in the future. He sees that she is investing in improving and perfecting their marriage and so feels total confidence in her.

Apologizing is a way for a wife to acknowledge her error and to benefit from it. As long as a person refuses to admit to herself that she has done something wrong or unacceptable, she cannot change her behavior for the better. Of course, it is easier to admit to oneself than to one's husband that a mistake has been made. However, if a wife can bring herself to share her remorse with her husband, she fulfills the important mitzvah of seeking forgiveness for the transgressions one commits between oneself and one's fellow man. (Even on Yom Kippur, atonement for such actions cannot occur in the absence of seeking forgiveness from the wronged person himself.)[26] In marriage, this mitzvah applies particularly to the categories of insulting or embarrassing another, damaging someone's person or property, and causing someone to suffer.[27] A wife can easily be guilty of all of these transgressions due to the intimate nature of her relationship with her husband. There will inevitably be quarrels and disagreements, short tempers and bad moods, misunderstandings and mistakes. It is thus essential for her own spiritual welfare, as well as for the good of the marriage, that she learn to apologize frequently and easily.

Apologizing causes a renewal to occur in the relationship. If a wife asks for forgiveness from her husband annually (on *erev* Yom Kippur, for example), it sets the tone for a fresh beginning and renewed optimism in the marriage. If she apologizes in the middle of a dispute, it gives the conversation a new turn and sets it on a constructive rather than destructive path.

Suppose a wife has answered her husband in a sarcastic and somewhat nasty fashion. As soon as she hears the words escape from her mouth, she regrets them; she sees that they are going to make matters worse rather than better. At this point, she can say, "Wait. Let me try that again. What I meant to say was...." or she can say, "I'm sorry. I didn't mean that. What I want to say is...." In other words, she can interrupt her tirade at midpoint and begin to communicate in a kind and caring fashion.

Even if several hours or days have gone by since a wife said or did something which she is now ashamed of, she can go back to her husband to rectify the situation. She can say, "I want to talk to you about yesterday. I'm sorry about the way I spoke to you. I've thought about it since, and I know that I should have said...." Of course, it is never too late to apologize for hurting your husband in any way. Even if years have gone by, if a wife has not yet apologized for a particular action, she can certainly do so. She needn't fear that bringing up an unpleasant subject will be harmful. On the contrary, her obvious concern for her husband and regret for her previous insensitivity will only enhance the relationship.

Example 1

wrong:

> wife: "I'm sorry I screamed at you, but you really deserved it! You just don't know when to stop provoking. How much patience can a person have?"

right:

> wife: "I shouldn't have raised my voice just then. I'm sorry. Let me try it again."

Example 2

wrong:

> husband: "You should wake Shmuley up in the morning instead of letting him sleep in longer than everyone else."

> wife: "I'm sorry. You're wrong. He's only a baby, and he needs his sleep."

Comment:

Naturally, it is important to apologize correctly. If the apology contains blame, as it does in the "wrong" dialogue in the first example, then it is not a sincere apology. It is missing the element of regret. Since the wife feels that her outburst is her husband's fault, she feels entitled to her own overreaction. She does not sincerely regret her lack of self-control. In fact, the wife should try to behave appropriately for the sake of improving the situation even if her husband provokes her. Moreover, she should accept responsibility for her own mistakes and endeavor to improve without waiting for her husband to take the first step. Blaming her husband is a way of not accepting responsibility, of not owning her own behavior. If she doesn't own her behavior, she can't apologize for it, nor can she improve it.

As we see in the second example, the words "I'm sorry" do not constitute an apology. Some people sprinkle many sentences with this expression where they have no intention of making apologies. As used in this example, the words indicate no regret. It is better to reserve the power of this important phrase for real occasions when you are genuinely sorry for something you've said or done. Overuse of these precious words detracts from their value when said at an appropriate moment.

30. Be Reasonable

An essential trait for the building of trust in marriage is being reasonable. This means that a wife will conduct herself in a basically normal, comprehensible fashion. Suppose she and her husband make plans to take the children to the museum one Sunday afternoon. When the time comes to leave, the wife announces that she's changed her mind. She doesn't want to go anymore. Naturally, the entire family will be disappointed. However, when her husband asks her for her reason, she just insists that she's not in the mood. If he persists, she gets annoyed and claims that she's entitled to change her mind. This sort of behavior is extremely unreasonable. Breaking a promise is bad enough, but refusing to explain oneself intelligently is cruel. Unreasonable behavior of this sort destroys trust in a marital relationship.

Unreasonable behavior is behavior which makes no sense. It is without "reason." In the literal sense, an unreasonable person offers no good reason for his or her actions; a wife who offers no explanation for her refusal to clean the house is being unreasonable. Certainly it is likely that she has a reason. It is her refusal to divulge it which breaks down communication and trust in her marriage.

Another type of unreasonable behavior is any exaggerated response. This includes becoming angry over minor incidents (screaming because someone dirtied a clean floor or didn't carry out a request exactly as demanded), sulking for hours after a disagreement (or refusing to make up for several days), becoming hysterical when something doesn't go the way it "should" have (showing utter lack of trust in *Hashem*), and any other inappropriate reaction to life's stresses and challenges. A husband cannot trust a wife who has not learned to bring her emotions under control. It is the task of every Jew to strive toward the happy medium in emotional behavior, facing life with a calm optimism and secure faith in *Hashem*.[28] Every wife must work on herself to achieve this state of emotional moderation in order to best influence her family and create a happy, healthy home environment. A mother who overreacts cannot help but harm her children as she goes about "making mountains out of molehills" and disciplining in an unreasonable manner. A husband who must witness his wife's inability to cope with the normal demands of child rearing, including dealing with misbehavior, immaturity, conflicts, behavior and learning problems, messes, inconveniences, and so on, not only loses trust in his wife, but also loses respect for her. Those women who claim they were not made for mother-ing because they lack patience simply have not yet decided to develop this important *middah*. We are all born with tenden-cies to emotional states—some of us anger quickly, some tend to be nervous, some are always bubbly and happy—it is our job to take what *Hashem* has endowed us with and bring it in line with Torah requirements. Unreasonable behavior is not the kind of behavior which the Torah advocates.

Example 1

wrong:

> husband: *"Why is Shmuli eating cookies so close to dinner time?"*
>
> wife: *"Because he's driving me crazy with his whining and cookies keep him quiet! I can't get anything done around here with that child in my way. He'll give me a heart attack one day!"*

right:

> husband: *"Why is Shmuli eating cookies so close to dinner time?"*
>
> wife: *"I gave them to him so he'd leave the kitchen. I know I probably shouldn't have, but it's the only thing that works when the kids aren't around to distract him. Have you got any better ideas for next time?"*

Example 2

wrong:

> husband: *"I really need a home computer for my business."*
>
> wife: *"We're not getting one."*
>
> husband: *"We can afford it with that bonus I just got at work."*

wife: "It's not that."

husband: "So what's the problem?"

wife: "I just don't want one in the house."

husband: "Why not?"

wife: "Could you please stop nagging me about this? I made my feelings clear and I don't want to be badgered any more."

husband: "You haven't made your feelings clear at all."

wife: "You just can't stop, can you?"

Comment:

A clue that someone is being unreasonable is use of extreme vocabulary. In the "wrong" dialogue of the first example, the wife uses several phrases which are escalatory in nature. They upset not only her husband, but herself as well. When we use emotionally charged language, we make things seem much worse than they are. Although it is true that the wife is having a hard time cooking with this toddler under her feet, this is not one of the most awful things that could happen in life. A sense of perspective is necessary, as is a sense of humor, when dealing with familial aggravations. In this case, the wife is being unreasonable in her excitable response to her husband's question. Moreover, she is working herself up (if she hasn't done so already) to an angry state, something which she should be trying to avoid.

In the "right" dialogue of this example, the wife admits that her strategy may not be the best choice, but she remains calm in the face of implied criticism and parental stress. She may not be smiling sweetly when she answers her husband's question, but she behaves in a normal fashion and does not "fly off the handle" because he questioned her judgment. Her moderate response is within reasonable range, reinforcing the development of basic trust within her marriage.

Example two illustrates the unreasonableness of a wife who won't explain her thinking processes. If she has no legitimate reason for her feelings, she can always say, "I don't know why I feel that way. It's just my reaction. It's not based on anything." This at least makes it clear that she herself is uncertain about the source of her feelings. However, pretending that she has given an acceptable explanation when she hasn't destroys trust in communication. The best approach is to have a reason for what we say and to explain that reason if called on to do so. "I'm entitled to my own feelings" is not a sentence geared to fostering marital trust and happiness. "I'll explain it as best as I can" is a sentence which brings husband and wife closer in mutual trust and affection.

Trust is an essential element of marriage. The above techniques can help foster the growth of trust. When a marriage is characterized by respect and trust, it is already a stable union. However, the true joy of marriage is not experienced unless strategies are developed for the maintenance of affection. The next section will outline some important techniques to achieve this goal.

CHAPTER FOUR
Developing and Maintaining Affection

In a Jewish marriage, one certainly expects to enjoy a relationship characterized by respectful interactions. However, we can really set our goals much higher. Each man and woman is entitled to a relationship filled with warmth and kindness, for kindness is the essence of all human interaction based on Torah principles. When the *aizer k'negdo* behaves in accordance with the laws of kindness, she creates the environment for the development of affection. Needless to say, her husband must also strive to behave in these same caring and careful ways if he wants to enjoy the affection of his wife. (As previously mentioned, a husband should ideally engage in ALL of the behaviors which are outlined in this manual for his wife.) However, a wife need not wait for her husband to show the initiative in this area. Since it is only natural to feel friendly and caring toward someone who acts in a friendly and caring way toward us, a wife who shows affection (consideration and kindness) toward her husband can increase the likelihood that he will respond with a similar feeling.

Despite the presence of an initial attraction, two people may find it hard to develop their love within the context of marriage. After all, marriage appears on the surface to be a rather mundane union. Two people live together, sharing space and responsibilities. They must negotiate finances, household chores, and child rearing duties. Sometimes their day seems to be a matter of taking out the garbage, cooking, cleaning up the kitchen, car-pooling, making *parnasah*, shopping, and disciplining. Husband and wife may operate on different schedules, barely passing each other in the course of a day. Rather than becoming ever closer, they may find themselves growing ever more distant, as their brief conversations focus increasingly on the business of their living arrangements ("What time do I need to take the children to the doctor?"—"I need more money for the food this week"—"Could you put your laundry in the basket instead of on the floor?"). The companionship and joy that characterizes good friendship can be absent from their relationship.

Although Jewish marriage may not be a romantic life style conducive to candlelight dinners and star gazing, it is definitely a structure in which feelings of warmth and love can grow and be maintained during the course of each busy, bustling day. The Torah instructs us about how to make this happen. Basically, *Hashem* commands us to conduct ourselves in such a

way that our spouse is likely to grow fond of us. We should
make ourselves pleasant and pleasing by our words and actions.[1] This means that even as we take out the garbage, wash
the dishes, and change the baby, we must be aware of our
power to build or destroy love. Each word we speak and action we do either contributes to the building of affection or to
the destruction of warm feelings. There is no neutral in human
interaction. Keeping this in mind, we can attempt to put a
smile on our face and a kind word in our mouth throughout
the course of our chores and actions. In fact, you will notice
that many of the techniques in this section stress the importance of being happy and positive in your outlook. Since this is
not a natural ability for most people, when we work on ourselves to be able to achieve this even partially, all of our mundane
actions then become elevated and filled with *kedushah*. The
rewards are both immediate and eternal as we reap the many
benefits of working toward *shalom bayis*.

Techniques

31. Make Your Arrivals and Departures Cheery

From *Pirkei Avos*[2] we learn that we should greet each person with a friendly smile. This act of kindness increases the
positive feelings others have toward us.[3] A wife should be
careful to be smiling and receptive when she first sees her husband at the end of the day. Knowing that a happy scene awaits
him, a husband looks forward to coming home. Similarly,
when husband and wife depart from each other in the morning, they should take care to wish each other a good day and
to be smiling and pleasant in their leave-taking. The words
spoken at this time create the last impression that each spouse

has of the other before each separation. A warm and friendly farewell from a wife gives a husband something to look forward to upon his return. On the other hand, strained and tense entrances and exits create aversion. A husband who knows that an unpleasant scene awaits him at home wishes to avoid coming home. If tension precedes his departure in the morning, he associates his wife with unhappiness. He draws away from her rather than closer to her.

Although all interactions during the day should be pleasant, arrivals and departures are particularly important because they set a tone for subsequent interactions. As we mentioned earlier, it is important to acknowledge your husband's entrance simply to be respectful. However, in order to actually build positive feelings, more than mere acknowledgment is required. A wife must remove herself from what she is doing (and she is always doing something) and put energy and enthusiasm into her greeting. Even if she doesn't feel relaxed and happy at that moment, she should plaster a smile on her face and make sure that her voice is upbeat and happy sounding. "Bye, Yosef! Have a great day! I'll speak to you later!"—"Hi, Yosef! I'm glad you're home. Did you have a nice day?" She need only be pleasant for sixty seconds, and then, when he's gone or not looking, she can revert to her miserable mood if she really wants to! She is simply making a sincere effort to increase marital affection by acting friendly for these brief moments. (Of course, there will be times when every woman is really too troubled or tense to try to smile. These times should, however, be very much the exception rather than the rule in her daily interactions.)

This technique is not only for new *kallahs*. It is appropriate for one hundred and twenty years of marriage. Each day is a day of marital renewal. Each day we must start again to win the love and affection of our mate. When we get too tired or nonchalant to do this, reducing our greetings to a perfunctory "bye" and "hi," we lose a valuable opportunity to increase warmth and affection in our marriage. As our interactions become mechanical and businesslike, so our emotions become dull and flat. There is no love without effort.

Example

wrong:

> *wife:* "Oh, you're home. Can you do something about these kids–they won't stop fighting. I can't finish my cooking with all this chaos."

right:

> *wife:* "Oh hi, Beryl! How are you? You look a little tired. Was traffic bad? I'm sorry dinner's a little delayed–the kids have been underfoot. Why don't you sit down and relax for a while while I finish off? Or better yet, read them all a story while you're waiting!"

Comment:

Which wife would YOU like to come home to? The wife in the "wrong" example is just behaving "naturally." She's tired from her struggle with the children and relieved that her husband is there to help. She acts out of a practical desire to get on with the business of preparing dinner. However, she is paying no attention to her marital relationship. She forgets that everything she says and does either enhances or detracts from her marital happiness. A tired husband cannot look forward to coming home to a frazzled, exhausted wife. Even though both have had hard days, they must gather the energy to be kind to each other. If they were courting, they would certainly manage to be pleasant no matter how fatigued they previously were. In fact, marital happiness could be ensured if the couple were to keep up their "courting" behaviors for the duration of their marriage.

The wife in the "right" example puts aside her activities and feelings in order to do the mitzvah of greeting her husband cheerfully and with kindness. She makes her marital relationship a priority and puts the practical issue of dinner preparation second on her list. After all, the business of running a home simply provides a setting in which *mitzvos* can be observed and love can be built. The purpose of the home is not to house and feed physical bodies, but rather to create a miniature *Beis HaMikdash* in which holiness resides. When a wife strives to fulfill her role as an *aizer k'negdo*, focusing on her spiritual task within the home, fulfilling all of the interpersonal *mitzvos* with her own husband, she elevates her dwelling into a place of *kedushah*. In order to do this, she must give her primary attention to the quality of her human interactions rather than to her household responsibilities. In practical terms, this means that taking time to greet her husband is more important than dusting and baking. The housework will get done in any event; marital affection will not grow without the proper attention.

32. Be Generous with Positive Communication

Positive communications are those interactions, verbal or nonverbal, which make a person feel good. A wife can be positive with her husband by speaking pleasantly to him, praising him, smiling at him, or doing something for him. Certainly most wives engage in these kinds of behaviors sometimes. However, in order to heighten affection between a man and wife, these behaviors must actually DOMINATE the relationship. In other words, the vast majority of the interactions that occur between the couple should be positive in nature. A wife should aim towards 80 percent positive behaviors—that is to say, eight out of every ten things she says or does should be endearing. Of course, she will sometimes have to make remarks which have a negative impact; she will not be able to avoid making the occasional critical statement or complaint, or even having to make an unpleasant request. However, these should be as rare as she can make them.

One form of positive communication which should be used frequently is the demonstration of gratitude. The Talmud states: "If you drank water from a well, do not throw stones at it."[4] The lesson is meant literally as well as metaphorically. If water has done us a favor by quenching our thirst, we should show our gratitude by not harming it, even if it is an inanimate object without feelings. How much more gratitude should we show a human being who has done us a kindness! Thus, a wife should accustom herself to saying "thank you" for everything her husband does for her, no matter how often he does it. For example, it may be his job to take out the garbage. He does it twice a week. Since he does it, she is relieved of doing this task. Therefore, she can mention her appreciation to him each time he's done his job. This is really no different than a husband thanking his wife each time she sets a meal before him. Even though it may be her "job" to do so (if that is the arrangement they've made) and even though she does so every day (perhaps three times a day), each meal requires effort on her part. She certainly deserves acknowledgment for that effort even though meal preparation is her responsibility.

Gratitude can be shown for any job that was performed by your husband simply to let him know that you appreciate his sense of responsibility and you notice his efforts on behalf of his family. This recognition will encourage him to continue to fulfill his duties while it makes him feel closer to you. Of course, gratitude should also be shown for all of those things your husband does just out of the kindness of his heart. For example, it may not be his "job" to clear the table, but if he decides to do it he should be generously thanked. A wife mustn't think to herself, "Why should I thank him? I myself clear the table thousands of times a year. It's about time he helped out!" Her resentful thoughts cannot bring her closer to her husband. Even if he missed many opportunities to be kind, when he finally does an act of *chessed* it should be welcomed graciously. How would we like it if *Hashem* had a begrudging attitude toward us, saying in effect, "She's finally doing a mitzvah! Why should I reward her? She should have done it long ago!" Moreover, if a wife desires that her husband behave in a thoughtful manner again, she should reinforce his be-havior with genuine praise and gratitude. If she ignores it, she may have to wait a long time before it is repeated.

Another important form of positive communication is the use of compliments. A sincere compliment is considered a great *chessed.*[5] When a wife compliments her husband, she increases his self-confidence and self-esteem. She makes him feel special and cherished. All people like to be told that they are attractive, competent, clever, needed, and loved. Since we ourselves like this sort of praise, we fulfill the mitzvah of "Love your fellow man as yourself" when we praise others.[6] A wife can drop remarks during the day about her husband's positive qualities: "I trust your judgment"—"That was a good decision"—"You're brilliant."—"That suit really looks nice on you"—"You're a great husband"—"I love when you take the kids out"—"I'm so proud of you." The list of possibilities is endless; a wife simply has to notice what her husband does right and be sure to comment on it. As she praises him, she increases his affection toward her. It is only natural to feel attracted to people who make you feel good. A wife who makes her husband feel good with her generous compliments develops affection within her marriage.

Example 1

wrong:

> *wife: "Chaim, I'm really glad you're getting your business in order. Now you're acting like a professional. I couldn't stand the way you were handling things before."*

right:

> *wife: "Chaim, I'm really glad you're getting your business in order. You're acting like a real professional!"*

Example 2

wrong:

> *wife: "What did the barber do to you?"*

right:

> *wife: "That's a new haircut! It makes you look younger."*

Comment:

There is a skill to delivering praise and compliments correctly. The desired effect of a "positive" comment is that it should make the person receiving it feel good inside. In the first example above, the wife tries to tell her husband that his new approach is great. When doing this the wrong way, she mentions that his previous approach was not to her liking. Thus, she is pairing a compliment with a criticism, something which we should always avoid. Even if someone says, "That suit looks much nicer than your old one," it may do more harm than good. The recipient of such a "compliment" may feel insulted or hurt at the remark about the old suit. There is no need to remind a person about a previous mistake or imperfection when praising his current behavior or appearance. In fact, the Torah cautions us against such behavior, teaching that when we praise someone, we must be careful not to mention or imply faults.[7] The wife correctly offers praise when she simply states what she likes without referring to what she didn't like before.

Another aspect of praising is searching for an honest statement that one can make in order to be encouraging. In the second example, the wife doing things the "wrong" way lets her husband know that his haircut is awful. Of course, he will feel very bad even if he seems to laugh off her comment. A husband likes his appearance praised even as much as a wife does! In the "right" response, the wife finds something pleasant she can say about the haircut without actually committing herself to liking it. She knows that the hair will soon grow back anyway, so soon she will be happy with his appearance again. It certainly does not enhance her marital relationship to make her husband feel bad, even if only mildly and briefly. On the other hand, gentle compliments can greatly facilitate the growth of affectionate feelings. It is not necessary to be honest about disapproving of something. For example, if a husband kindly made dinner and it was not very tasty, there would be no need to say so. In fact, such a comment would be quite hurtful. A wife could praise his thoughtfulness in making dinner or the obvious trouble he went to. If he insists on knowing if she likes the food, she can say she likes anything that he makes for her. If she really finds it objectionable, she can say, "Even though I wouldn't ask for this dish again, I want you to know I really appreciate your making dinner tonight. It was so great knowing I didn't have to do that chore when I was already exhausted. You're a great husband." However, this kind of comment would be necessary only if the husband insisted on knowing whether she enjoyed the food itself. Her goal is always to be kind with her words, increasing the warm feelings between herself and her husband.

33. Refrain from Excessive Criticism

The Baal Shem Tov said: "'Love your fellow man as yourself.' You know that you have many faults, nevertheless, you still love yourself. That is how you should feel toward your friend. Despite his faults, love him."[8] When we love someone while being aware of their faults, we take care not to hurt them. For example, a mother may know that her youngster tends to be impulsive, self-centered, and introverted. She knows that he has many other minor faults as well. Nonetheless, she treats him kindly, does many things for him, and shows him clearly that she loves him dearly. She doesn't reject him because he has faults.

However, when a woman sees that her husband has faults (and every husband has faults, of course, as does every wife!), she may feel that this makes him less lovable. She feels that she will only be able to truly love him when he improves. In other words, when he loses twenty-five pounds, stops being selfish, takes more responsibility in household chores, and so on—then she will be able to love him. In order to bring that day closer, she actively works to see that he does improve. She corrects and criticizes his behavior hoping that he'll heed her words and change for the better.

Such a woman is making two mistakes. The first is her assumption that her husband is not lovable until he changes. True, there may be a husband who behaves so badly in so many areas that his wife really cannot tolerate him. The pain he causes her is simply too great. Moreover, it is not counterbalanced by a number of redeeming characteristics. In this case, the husband would have to become a lovable person in order to win the love of his mate. A truly patient *aizer k'negdo* can sometimes be successful in helping a man make this sort of transformation. The Midrash tells of a man who married a bad woman and became bad and a woman who married a bad man and made him good. The story illustrates that a woman has the power to change her spouse for better or worse.[9] Certainly, she should try her best to influence him positively before giving up on the possibility of happiness. Rabbinic and psychological counseling may be helpful.

Baruch Hashem, truly unlovable husbands are extremely rare (as are unlovable wives). Usually such people are suffering from some form of psychological disturbance which requires correction. The vast majority of husbands consists of normal people who have strengths and weaknesses. These people are lovable simply because *Hashem* has "said" so. The Holy One, blessed be He, said: "My beloved children, do I lack anything that I have to ask you for it? All I ask is that you love and honor each other. Nothing more!"[10]

Thus, if a woman has a husband who is basically normal, she can expect that she will be happy with some of his behaviors and not so pleased with others. She can and should love him even while being aware that he has faults. This brings us to the second error made by the type of wife described above. Her mistake is in thinking that she can help her husband change by criticizing and correcting him. While a woman may desire to help her husband change in certain areas (especially areas which affect her directly, such as laziness in making *parnasah*, failure to discipline the children, or refusal to help her with household tasks), she needs to be very careful about HOW she goes about "helping" him. She particularly needs to understand the effect of criticism.

How does it feel when YOU are criticized? Suppose you make a kugel for the family for Shabbos. Everyone takes a bite and then tells you what is wrong with it: "Too salty"—"Too mushy"—"Too dried out"—"Tasteless." You understand clearly that they aren't happy with it. Do you feel like trying to make it again? Let's say you decide to give it another try. This time they say, "It looks funny"—"Why can't you buy us some instead?"—"I hate this stuff!"—"Couldn't you add more sugar or something?" Now how do you feel? Most people feel like giving up. A lot of women would simply decide that they aren't good at making kugel and would not want to try anymore. If it took you time and trouble to prepare the dish, you might also feel hurt or angered by all of the negative feedback. You may not feel particularly warm and friendly toward your critics.

Now imagine how it would have been if your kugel was well received: "Delicious!"—"Wow, could you make this every week?"—"It's just perfect!"—"I love the crispy topping!" Now you likely feel terrifically encouraged and ready to zip back to the kitchen to make more and more kugels. Moreover, you feel happy in the presence of your admirers. You feel closer to them. This is the result of positive interactions. Emotionally, they increase affection. Cognitively, they lead to confidence. Success breeds success. Failure leads to frustration and giving up. The normal effect of criticism on human beings is that it causes discouragement and avoidance. Praise and compliments lead to increased effort and improved performance.

Thus, if a wife says to her husband, "If you're going to clear the table like that, I might as well do it myself," his feeling will be, "Then do it yourself. Why should I try when I'm obviously not good at this job." In other words, his experience of failure makes him want to give up. (This is all the more so when a person did not really care for the job in the first place.) In addition, he will feel resentful toward his wife because of her criticism. Instead of drawing close to her, he moves further from her. Affection is weakened with every critical comment one makes.

To illustrate just how sensitive men are to critical, nagging, correcting wives, let us examine some Talmudic quotations:

"An evil woman is worse than death." (In death, you die once, with an evil woman, you die over and over again.)[11]

"An evil woman is compared to hell itself."[12]

"A man ages prematurely from a bad-tempered wife."[13]

"He who is ruled by his wife has no life."[14]

Of course, these statements may refer to wives whose faults are greater than just being critical, but a critical tendency in a spouse can certainly lead to the kind of unhappiness described here. Constant criticism destroys harmony and affection in a marriage.

If this is so, how can a woman help her husband to change his behavior when it needs changing for the sake of marital happiness? There are, in fact, many techniques she can use. One important one described throughout this book is the simple use of modeling. By behaving in the correct and desirable manner herself, she demonstrates repeatedly how a person should behave in certain situations. With the passage of years, a husband automatically becomes more like his wife by living with her and observing her. (Some spouses even start to look like each other after a while because they begin to use similar facial expressions and body movements.) Of course, this route to change is very slow and requires much patience. Nonetheless, an *aizer k'negdo* uses this technique frequently.

Another strategy for inducing change is the use of positive reinforcement. Whenever a husband performs in a way which even approaches a desired behavior (e.g., clears the table but does so inadequately), the wife is sure to offer praise and encouragement ("Oh, thank you so much for helping! I really appreciate it! Since you took off all the big things, I only need to clear the cutlery and glasses—that's a big help"). Since the husband will feel his efforts were successful, he will be inclined to make more efforts and more improvements. He will also feel closer to his wife.

Another useful technique is to make straightforward requests for change: "Could you please chew a little quieter?" All such requests should be phrased in terms of the desirable behavior—ask for what you want. Do not say what you don't like (e.g., "You're chewing too loudly"). Say, "Could you help me put the kids to bed from now on?" (not: "You never help me put the kids to bed") and "I'd like it if you could spend more time with me" (not: "You don't spend enough time with me"). This lesson is taught in *Tanach* in the section in which Yisro advises Moshe how to improve a situation. Instead of just complaining about his management techniques, he makes constructive suggestions.[15]

A fourth technique for improving someone's behavior is to enlist the help of a third party. Children are useful for this. Suppose a husband mumbles his *benching* after meals. Instead of correcting and criticizing ("Shlomoh, can't you *bench* loudly and clearly?"), the wife says to the children, "Show your father how beautifully you *bench*." The sweet voices of the little darlings can inspire the husband to do better himself. Another use of "third parties" is consultation with a Rav or counselor. This technique should be used after all positive strategies have been exhausted and still no change is apparent in an area of MAJOR concern. In other words, some behaviors will not change, but they need not threaten the happiness or stability of the marriage. Some examples are a husband who never learns to throw his clothes in the laundry basket, one who chews his food too loudly, or one who doesn't like to travel. Although these may be unpleasant characteristics for some women to live with, a wife could learn to tolerate them in a husband who has redeeming characteristics (involves himself in mitzvah observance, is a good provider, is a good father, has a wonderful sense of humor, is kind, etc.). If, however, the behavior in question seriously affects the relationship (e.g., a husband who radically different religious values from his wife's, one who is an alcoholic, one who refuses to make *parnasah*, one who has a dangerously violent temper, etc.), then all efforts need to be made to change the behavior. What constitutes an area of major concern is peculiar to each woman. A wife must decide for herself whether she can or cannot live with a certain fault. When necessary, she can then urge her husband to come with her for counseling to help resolve important issues which they have not been able to resolve on their own.

Is there a time when criticism is appropriate? Yes. Criticism can be helpful when it is offered very RARELY and when it is done in a gentle, positive manner when both the criticizer and the "criticizee" are in good moods (not angry, tired, ill, or upset). In addition, it must be possible for the husband to make improvements as a result of the criticism. For example, there is no point in telling him that his socks don't match when he's out at a wedding with you and can't return home to change them. The time for such a comment is only when he's still at home. Otherwise the result of the criticism is, since no change can occur, that the husband will feel uncomfortable the rest of the evening. Since the wife has made this negative remark, she pushes her husband further from her (all negative comments have this effect). Moreover, she is wasting her precious ration of criticisms. A wife can only use a limited number of criticisms per day without destroying her marital happiness. To a certain extent, the number depends on her husband's sensitivity. It might be anywhere from three to five. Zero is a nice number to aim for, since this often results in lowering the actual number considerably. It is a good idea to keep a record of the number of criticisms you now give on an average day to see if any adjustment is necessary. Remember, the fewer criticisms you give, the more potent each one is. Repetitive criticisms (called "nagging") result in a husband who is "deaf" to all complaints.

Example

wrong:

> *wife:* "*You never defend me in front of the children. Whenever they tell you their stories, you take their side against me. Why do you always believe them? How do you think it makes me feel? You're destroying their respect for their mother, you know, which only hurts them in the long run. You're hurting them as well as me by this kind of behavior.*"

right:

> *wife:* "*I'd like you to defend me in front of the children when there is a dispute between them and myself. I feel really hurt when you take sides with them against me, and I'm concerned that they will lose respect for me.*"

Comment:

There are many problems with this criticism in the "wrong" example. The first one is that it is much too long. When a complaint is lengthy, it is perceived as a lecture. People "turn off" lengthy tirades, not listening past the first sentence or two. At that point they simply become defensive and resistant. Any criticism you make should be no more than one or two sentences long.

A second problem is that the criticism takes the form of a personal attack. The wife is giving "you messages" which state what is wrong with "you" (in this case, her husband). A "you message" says YOU are wrong, bad, incompetent, or whatever. A more effective, constructive, and endearing approach is to use the "I message." An "I message" states "my" feelings (in this case, the wife's): "I feel hurt"—"I'm disappointed"—"I'd like your co-operation." The "I message" can also say what you want from your spouse.

A third problem with the criticism is that it is obviously spoken in anger. When a wife rants and raves, she weakens her point significantly while managing to lose the affection of her husband simultaneously! Of course there are times when a wife simply cannot control her anger (although she should always strive to),[16] but she should not choose such moments to make a serious statement to her husband about a behavior that requires improvement. It would be better for her to walk around the block fifteen times, write an essay (to be torn up when completed), or go shopping than to speak to her husband in the midst of her anger. Only when she is calm again should she attempt to communicate with him about an important issue.

In all cases, a wife should evaluate how important it is to make a particular critical statement. She should set priorities in her mind for the things that bother her about her husband's behavior. Then she can criticize those things which are at the "top" of her list and let many minor annoyances pass. Treating every fault as if it were a major problem results in excessive criticism and excessive unhappiness. It destroys marital affection.

34. Spend Quality Time with Your Husband

"Quality time" is that time of day which is utilized to create and maintain affection in marriage. Ideally, every interaction you have with your husband can be described as "quality time" because every interaction can contribute to building marital harmony if you want it to. Thus, a wife can make a point to smile, speak in a pleasant tone of voice, use praise and compliments in her speech, and so on in order to endear herself to her husband. She can do this even while she is negotiating business matters with him, such as who will do car pool, who will rake up the leaves, or whether there is enough money to purchase a new rug.

Another type of quality time is the longer time span reserved for non-business interaction. In this sort of quality time, husband and wife take time to relate as friends rather than just as business partners. They put aside their "business" of household management issues and focus on each other as people. In this way, they create an opportunity to appreciate each other as unique individuals who are interesting and lovable in themselves and not just useful because of their functions in the marriage. So much of a married day consists of husband and wife pursuing their individual responsibilities—studying, making money, cooking, cleaning, shopping, child care—that many of their interpersonal interactions center around these functions. A wife talks to her husband about picking up clothes from the cleaners and he talks to her about a bill that must be paid. They forget how to talk to each other about life, about *Hashem*, about their goals and dreams, their interests and joys. Thus, they cease to be friends and do not experience the joys and rewards of friendship.

This is not the way Jewish marriage is meant to be. A wife is described as being a true friend to her husband: "And she is your companion, the wife of your covenant."[17] She is not a servant or business partner, but an intimate companion. *Chazal* say that the relationship between husband and wife should be characterized by a personal, congenial companionship.[18] They should enjoy light conversation and humor as do the closest of friends.[19] This may not come about naturally within a marriage, but requires effort and planning in many cases. A wife can help by making herself available for quality time.

For example, dinner time can be quality time if both parties agree that no business is to be discussed at the table. This may be better for digestion as well as for the marital relationship! Words of Torah may be spoken, and topics of interest, ideas, and experiences can be shared and discussed. However, no problems should be raised, no difficult issues brought forth, no arrangements made, or aggravations discussed. All of these kinds of negotiations should be reserved for a later point in the day—at the business meeting that you schedule to discuss such things. You might have a regular time scheduled each day (such as noon hour, 6:30 p.m., or 9:00 p.m.) to make plans and arrangements and problem solve. Some people find that once a week is enough for this sort of activity. The time frame itself should be brief, no more than ten to fifteen minutes.

For some couples, dinner time provides enough quality time per day. Some people also find it possible to take the first five minutes after the husband comes home. They ask the children to busy themselves for this short time while the parents talk. Others may like to schedule an evening meeting in which to relax together, learn, talk, or share some project. Again, the time period itself can be brief, say, ten to twenty minutes. However, during that time, a wife relates to her husband as a companion, a friend. The pressures of their daily life are temporarily lifted, and they simply enjoy each other's company and support. An arrangement of this sort does much to create and maintain affection in marriage. If it is not consciously planned, however, days, weeks, and years can go by without husband and wife finding time to enjoy each other. Naturally, the effects on marital happiness are quite negative.

Example 1

wrong:

husband *(calling his wife on the phone):* "Hi, Bayla. Any messages?"

wife: "Mr. Abrams called."

husband: "O.K. I'll be home soon."

wife: "Bye."

right:

husband: "Hi, Bayla. Any messages?"

wife: "Hi, Moshe. Mr. Abrams called. How are things going?"

husband: "Fine. I'm really busy today."

wife: "Me too. I've been on the phone all morning trying to organize car pools for the kids. At least I've got two done and only two more to do."

husband: "That's great. Keep up the good work. I'll be home soon."

wife: "That's nice. The kids can't wait to see you. Drive carefully."

Example 2

wrong:

husband: "So, here we are for quality time. What's new?"

wife: "Nothing. What's new with you?"

husband: "Nothing."

wife: "Well, I guess that's it for quality time tonight."

husband: "I guess so."

right:

> *husband: "So, here we are for quality time. What's new?"*
>
> *wife: "Did I tell you I love you today?"*
>
> *husband: "No, I don't think you mentioned anything about that."*
>
> *wife: "Well, I do. I'm really glad we got married. You're a great person."*
>
> *husband: "Hey, I like this quality time!"*

Comment:

Quality time can be incorporated into many conversations and interactions you have throughout the day. Telephone calls can be utilized to increase affection, or they can be just another "business" dealing between husband and wife. Although it may not be appropriate to have lengthy conversations by phone (perhaps the husband is in a busy office environment, is in a situation which lacks privacy, or is pressured for time), it is usually possible to speak four or five brief but pleasant sentences to each other. If there is not time for even that, it might be better not to make the call at all because the pressure can lead to unpleasant rushed and curt interactions which reduce affection.

"Quality" telephone conversations can be particularly challenging for a busy housewife with youngsters underfoot. Often the little ones choose to beg for Mommy's attention when they see she is on the phone. This may make it hard for her to relax and give her husband the attention which would make him feel close to her. Nonetheless, if she concentrates on making just two or three pleasant remarks (even while her little sweethearts climb up her legs or spill cereal on each other), she has made a significant contribution to the creation of warmth and friendship in her marriage. She can always end the conversation in a friendly fashion by saying, "I'd better hang up now. Your lovely children are calling. We all look forward to seeing you soon!" All of this takes only a matter of seconds. However, this small investment yields great dividends in terms of marital closeness.

Example two shows a potential problem of scheduled quality time: people don't know how to fill it. As is shown in the "right" dialogue, even if a wife has no new ideas or thoughts to share she can always give positive affirmations during this period. It always contributes to marital harmony to let your spouse know how great you think he is! Nonetheless, if a couple routinely finds they have nothing to talk about during this time, they should endeavor to schedule an activity they can do together or a specific topic they can learn about or discuss. Planning for quality time can help a couple look forward to being with each other and can, in fact, enhance the actual time spent together when it comes.

35. Create an Impression of Contentment

It is important for a wife to appear (in general) as if she is happy. Of course, it is a Torah obligation to actually be happy ("You shall rejoice with all the good that the Almighty has given you").[20] Many people do not realize that their emotional state has a very large impact on those they live with. If a wife is depressed, she brings that depression into her home and into her relationship with her husband and children. Everyone feels "down" around her. On the other hand, the presence of a joyful person cheers people up. Happiness is contagious. Thus, it is considered an act of kindness to be happy around other people.[21]

In *Pirkei Avos* we learn that we should "welcome everyone with a joyful countenance."[22] A pleasant facial expression is considered equal to giving a person the most treasured gifts in the world.[23] It is thus clear that a wife gives her husband something very valuable when she simply smiles at him and acts happy around him. Although it is neither possible nor necessary for wives to be constantly in a joyous mood, many women are not careful enough to present an image of basic contentment to their spouses.

During the courting stage of their relationship, almost all women manage to put on a happy face. They realize that others are not attracted to depressed people or those whose main occupation is whining or complaining. However, once they are married, these same ladies feel that they no longer have to put on appearances. They can look and sound miserable if they feel that way. They are forgetting their own wisdom: men do not want to be around unhappy women. This does not mean that a wife can never look less than joyous! It means only that her USUAL countenance should be relatively peaceful and pleasant rather than harried, tense, depressed, angry, or otherwise negative.

When a husband calls during the day to ask how things are going, he doesn't necessarily want to hear only about the trials and tribulations you are having. When discussing the day's events over dinner, he also won't enjoy hearing only about the problems you are having at work, at home, with friends, and with family. Most people simply don't enjoy hearing so much bad news. Moreover, the more your partner hears about all the things that go wrong in your life and how people don't treat you properly, the less respect he will have for you. What Rav Ovadiah Bartenurah states for the husband—"If he confides in her and tells her that his friends mocked him, then she too will scorn him in her heart"[24]—applies equally to the wife. Nobody wants an incompetent marriage partner. Thus, a wife should be sure to balance her reports with happy stories, funny interludes, enjoyable experiences, and the like. In other words, she should share her UPS and downs with her spouse—not just the downs!

What if you really are unhappy, however? What if you do have serious issues that you need to discuss, or at least get off your chest? This happens to all people at various times. There are bound to be certain periods in your life when you have trouble being upbeat, relaxed, and happy. Providing these times are restricted to infrequent, temporary occasions, they do no serious harm to the marital relationship. Normal marital partners are glad to be there in times of need, offering support and encouragement. However, if the problems are chronic and ongoing, if they actually characterize your style of relating, then your husband will have trouble seeing you through each one. A husband has no desire to be a psychiatrist for his wife; he wants a mature, healthy, coping adult for his life partner. If you are consistently troubled or unhappy, personal counseling may be advisable to help you achieve greater contentment. It is, however, unreasonable to expect your husband to be willing or able to help you overcome serious emotional problems or feel warmth and closeness to you when you are consistently depressed or troubled.

Sometimes a wife has no serious emotional problem, yet finds herself irritated or upset frequently. Perhaps she has a difficult job, difficult children, or some other difficult situation in her life. Every day she suffers from the difficulty, so that she tends to look and feel unhappy much of the time. At first, her husband may be sympathetic to her plight. As time goes on, however, he may become impatient with her inability to "get on with things" and be happy. He starts to enjoy her company less and less. The woman's problems do not warrant consultation with a Rav or counselor, but she doesn't want to burden her husband daily with her complaints and concerns. What can she do? She can spread out her need to complain. Instead of repeating herself endlessly to her husband, let her also complain to one special friend. She can call or visit with this companion, discuss her aggravations and issues, and seek advice and support. Since this friend does not live in the same house with her, she will be less affected by the negative mood of the wife. Moreover, there are certain people who enjoy helping others gain perspective and insight into their problems (would-be psychologist types). They themselves may be unhappy and glad to help in the spirit of "misery loves company," or they may be very well adjusted and simply inclined toward chessed. Whatever their motivation, they are a better source of comfort than her own husband because they are not dependent on the wife for anything. If they should tire of the negative nature of their interactions, they may withdraw their friendship eventually. The wife can usually replace one good listener with another fairly easily. What is harder to replace is a good husband. However, this sort of wife will not lose her husband's affection since she is careful to maintain an impression of contentment in her dealings with him (balancing happy tidings with unhappy ones) and shares her daily, repetitive dissatisfactions with her lady friend. Such a wife does maintain communication with her husband about all issues of importance and concern to her; she simply is careful not to repetitively harp on old issues. In the course of their marriage, she is trying to earn his love and affection in the same way she tried to win it before they were married. She is trying to be a positive person.

Example 1

wrong:

> *husband: "Hi, Devorah. I'm home."*
>
> *wife: "Oy, you wouldn't believe what kind of day I've had."*

right:

> *husband: "Hi, Devorah. I'm home."*
>
> *wife: "Oh hi, Avraham. I'm glad you're back. Do you have time to have a cup of tea with me for a few minutes? The children are playing outside and I'd really enjoy relaxing with you for a little while."*

Example 2

wrong:

> *husband: "Hi. How are you? How were the children today?"*
>
> *wife: "Fine. Everyone was fine."*
>
> *husband: "You don't look too happy about it."*
>
> *wife: "I told you everything was fine. If you're going to get pushy about it, I'll tell you the truth–everything was awful!"*

right:

> *husband: "Hi. How are you? How were the children today?"*
>
> *wife: "Now that you're home, we're all fine! Let's have dinner and relax a little."*

Comment:

No doubt the husband has also had a challenging day. Who doesn't? There is no point in complaining to each other about the same problems every day. Certainly if some new issue arises it may be worth discussing, but the regular daily problems can be avoided. Instead of ruminating over the day's disasters and re-experiencing the negative emotions that occurred ("It was just terrible when the kids wouldn't stop fighting—I had my friend over and I was so embarrassed"), a wife can take time to build affection with her husband and turn to him as a source of strength and joy after a hard day.

In the "right" dialogue of the first example, the wife wants to sit and enjoy her husband's company. If she did in fact have a hard day, she finally has an opportunity to unwind and engage in the pleasurable activity of being with the one she loves. She can make this a time for re-energizing, gathering strength from the pleasant interlude to carry on with her responsibilities and challenges. If she uses this time only to describe all the things that went wrong, she will probably feel drained and unhappy after her "break." What a waste of an opportunity to refresh oneself and build affection simultaneously!

The "wrong" wife in the second example tries to hide her gloomy mood by telling her husband that everything was fine. Her face and tone of voice give her away, however. Rather than pretend that a bad day was a good day, a wife should concentrate on the reality that the bad part seems to be over and everything at the present moment is, in fact, fine. If things are not fine at the moment the husband makes his inquiry, the wife can still be honest in her response: "I'm having a hard time, but the kids will be in bed soon, and I'm really looking forward to relaxing with you later. Maybe you can settle them down a bit while I get myself a cup of tea." She needn't go into the gory details of all of the squabbles and unpleasant interactions that have been going on. Her orientation is still toward a better time coming up (if it is not already happening). A husband doesn't expect to see his wife dancing for joy when he comes home; he only likes to know that she can cope with life's challenges optimistically and that she is basically content despite the normal hardships of daily living.

36. Do Things for Your Husband

When we do something for someone, we develop a feeling of closeness toward them. This fact is the motivating principle behind the prohibition of acts of intimacy when a wife is in the *niddah* state.[25] At such times, a wife must be careful NOT to do certain acts of kindness for her husband, lest they lead to physical intimacy. For example, she may not serve him food or drink, nor may she prepare his bed or water for washing in his presence.

Thus, one way that a wife can foster the growth of affection between herself and her husband is to do things for him. Besides the reward of increasing marital love, she receives the reward for doing the mitzvah of kindness—for kindness is one of the three things on which the world exists.[26] Even if her husband inadvertently fails to notice her efforts, *Hashem* never fails to record them.

What sorts of things can a wife do for her husband? Doesn't she already do quite enough by virtue of rearing his children and keeping his house in order? Every dinner she makes is certainly an act of kindness, as is every button she sews and every pleasant word she speaks. What more does she need to do?

Oddly enough, a man does not usually love his wife because she fulfills these kinds of functions for him. In fact, while a wife works away, polishing and shining and organizing, she may not realize that her husband has long since lost affection for her. She may think to herself, "See what a good wife I am? See how I do everything here and keep this place running smoothly? My husband is a lucky man!" Yet the husband thinks, "I wish my wife were kinder to me. All day she screams at me to take my shoes off, hang my coat up, clean up after myself. Nag, nag, nag. Why can't I come home to a sweet and loving wife?" Of course, housework does not have to be an area of contention between husband and wife, although it very often is. Even when it is not, however, most men simply do not say to themselves, "My wife does such a wonderful job taking care of the home and family that I truly love her!" Nor do women say, "My husband does such a wonderful job of supporting us that I truly love him!" Only when a wife fails to do an adequate job in the area of her domestic responsibilities, or when a husband fails to do an adequate job in his areas, do marital partners notice (and complain). After all, when the house is clean, people don't notice—but when it's messy they will.

Of course, ingratitude is not acceptable Torah behavior.[27] A husband really SHOULD appreciate and acknowledge his wife's efforts on his behalf, and she should appreciate and acknowledge his, even when these efforts seem only to be the expected responsibilities of each spouse. Nonetheless, carrying out one's responsibilities in itself does not build affection.

Personal acts of kindness, on the other hand, do. What constitutes, then, a "personal act of kindness"?

This is any behavior done specifically for your husband simply to make him smile. For example, writing him a cute poem when you have to leave a message can be a nice touch ("I hope you're fine, I'll be back at nine, help yourself to the cheese and wine"). You don't have to be Shakespeare in order to do these things; just do whatever comes naturally for you. Some people might draw an illustration to go with a note to evoke a smile. Others can make a joke within the note itself. Others can put a serious but loving touch to a memo ("I'll be back at nine. I miss you already!"). Some wives like to put a tender thought in the lunch bag—a pleasant surprise for a husband to find along with his egg salad sandwich. A lot can be done with a message pad!

Another endearing technique is to pick up a small treat for your spouse. This can range anywhere from unhealthy but delicious sweets (donuts, chocolate bars, croissants, etc.) to small items and utensils which he might not buy for himself (a particular book, the perfect screwdriver, a new tie, a pen that works, his own pad of paper, etc.). Less costly treats include special books from the library and homemade delicacies. Anything that he doesn't expect is eligible for this category. If you can picture his smile upon receipt of the item, it's the right thing.

Another act of personal kindness is to ask him what he'd really like for dinner once in a while and then make it for him even if the children don't like it (you can always serve them spaghetti that night!). Similarly, if he tells you that he likes a certain dress on you, be sure to wear it around him whenever you can. You can ask him who he'd like to have as a Shabbos guest and invite that person; what he'd like to do on *motzo'ei* Shabbos and then do it with him; where he'd like to go on an outing and then agree to go. In other words, ask him what would make him happy and then do it for him.

These techniques go beyond the call of duty. Their purpose is to increase the husband's affection for his wife as he receives this positive attention from her and to increase her affection for him as she involves herself in doing things for him. Thus, these special efforts can be crucial elements in building and maintaining marital affection.

Example

wrong:

> *wife: "Why should I go out of my way for him? He never does anything like that for me. The last time he brought me flowers was before we were married. He forgets my birthday unless I remind him. He certainly doesn't do anything special or thoughtful for me during the year. Even on Yom Tov he forgets to buy me something–after he reviews the* halachos *about gladdening your wife!"*

Comment:

An *aizer k'negdo* cannot look at her husband's behavior and decide that he doesn't merit her efforts. Her essential task is to lead him to a higher plane of functioning through her example and efforts. When she starts to treat him in a special, caring way, giving him little doses of personalized attention and love, he will learn how to emulate this sort of behavior as well. Even if he hasn't yet caught on (e.g., ten years into the marriage), never despair. He might surprise you yet. Even if he never catches on, your marriage will still benefit because these acts of kindness will draw him close to you. He may have trouble giving gifts, but he may demonstrate his love for you in other ways. Be careful to observe the ways in which he does demonstrate his caring. People have different styles. If necessary, ask him if he notices and appreciates your efforts, and tell him that you'd like him to tell you about it and even to reciprocate. In almost all cases, a husband will respond to such a direct request. However, if after you treat him lovingly and kindly for a very long time, he appears, Heaven forbid, not to care for you, consultation with your Rav or counselor would be in order.

37. Make Things Humorous and Light

Whenever possible a wife should bring a little humor into her dealings with her husband. Humor brings people closer together, relaxes them, and makes them happy. When humor is used for this purpose, it is considered a great mitzvah, an act of kindness. The story is told in the Gemara about two men in a marketplace who were deemed worthy of receiving a portion in the World To Come. Their merit was that they were humorists who made people happy and who ended quarrels between people by joking with them.[28] A wife can also cheer her husband up and cause him to feel close to her when she employs the techniques of humor.

Some women may feel that they are unable to be funny with their husbands. Some are careful not to be exceedingly frivolous in general for fear of transgressing the directives of our Sages who caution us against this.[29] However, the warning refers to purposeless frivolity—being light-headed and foolish to the point of excess (something like being drunk).

This sort of attitude prevents proper spiritual development. However, when humor has a purpose, when it is used for the sake of developing *shalom bayis* and bringing joy into a household, it is not only permissible, but desirable. In fact, the Gemara illustrates that humor can be used to increase affection and intimacy when it relates the story of Rav who was overheard conversing frivolously with his wife before having relations.[30]

Moreover, women should remember that joyfulness has been decreed by *Hashem* Himself: "And you shall rejoice before the Lord, Your God."[31] Expressing joy involves looking happy, smiling, and laughing. Again, this is not the empty laughter of pleasure-seekers, but rather the joy one experiences from doing *mitzvos*, from living a wholesome Jewish life. *Hashem* loathes a depressed attitude so much that it is written: "The Divine Presence does not rest upon anyone unless he is joyful."[32] Joyfulness is a skill which can be learned and practiced rather than being an innate disposition. A wife who wants to develop this skill must learn to think in positive ways, replacing depressing or worrisome thoughts with happy and confident ones. We have control over what we put into our minds. We can choose not to permit negative ideas to float around inside us, and we can choose to fill our brains with pleasant and happy thoughts. We can force our faces to smile and our mouths to speak pleasant words. We can even learn to joke and make others laugh. After a time, these behaviors and thought patterns become part of us rather than being imposed artificially. As for those women who claim they have no talent in the humor department—watch how they get along with their women friends. The majority of women talking with each other know very well how to banter and joke and enjoy themselves. The park benches are filled with laughing mothers watching their youngsters and conversing happily with each other. Even when discussing important philosophical and religious issues, they have the ability to bring lightness and humor into the conversation. This ability can also be used with one's husband.

It is not necessary to spend large amounts of time each day in idle chatter with one's husband, and the Torah advises us against such interactions.[33] However, even "serious" conversations can contain an element of humor. Certain activities (such as taking family photographs) actually lend themselves to a good use of humor. Passing comments can be made light and funny as well. There should be enough humor to create a feeling of comfort and joy in the home—but not so much that it threatens the spiritual well-being of the family.

There are some things that a wife can do to bring an element of humor into the relationship without having to make quips and jokes. For example, if she comes across a relevant cartoon or joke in a magazine or newspaper, she can stick it up on the fridge. (Often a serious point can be made in this way without causing offence to anyone.) The children may bring work from school that is funny and endearing, which can also be posted in a prominent location. Pictures taken of the family members in natural poses with great big smiles can be hung in a place which is passed many times a day. A bulletin board containing a "happy thought for the day" or even a "funny thought for the day," culled from some library collection of such thoughts, can also be utilized.

The important thing is to create an atmosphere which is light and gay in your household. Each woman can do this in her own way.

Examples

wrong:

> *wife:* "Your dinner was just great, Yossi. The kids can take the leftovers to school to use as paste."

wrong:

> *wife:* "Don't look so serious, Dovid. I didn't mean it when I said I didn't love you as much as you love me. Can't you take a joke?"

wrong:

> *wife:* "Let's hide your father's watch from him and see how long it takes for him to notice it's missing."

wrong:

> *wife:* "Don't worry about not fixing the fridge, Chaim. I know you never do what you say you will, so I called the repairman this morning. It only cost two million dollars, but it was worth it to save me nagging you a whole week!"

Comment:

A joke is defined as funny only when everyone truly enjoys it. If some people are laughing at the expense of others, cruelty has replaced humor. A wife should never say anything that will hurt her husband. Sometimes people use "jokes" to cover up nasty communications. They use sarcasm and bitter humor when they are really trying to make a serious statement. Never try to be funny when you have something important to say! Save the laughter for a lighter moment in your lives.

Sarcasm can be particularly hurtful and destructive to the formation of positive feelings in marriage. Observe the following interaction:

husband: *"Could you please serve me a second helping of cholent, Chayah?"*

wife: *"Why? Did your arms fall off?"*

What the wife might be trying to say is that the cholent pot is closer to her husband than it is to her, and she would appreciate it if he would help himself since she is eating, or tired, or otherwise unavailable to serve right then. Why doesn't she just say this instead of making a nasty "joke," which can only increase distance between her and her spouse? Learning to be "straight"—say what we mean in a straightforward fashion—is one of the most important marriage techniques.

When humor is used in conversation, it should be obvious that laughter and good feelings are the intended results. The phrase "I was only joking" should not have to be used. If you made a joke it should be self-evident so that you don't have to explain you were joking. "I was only joking" is never an excuse for causing someone pain. It does not undo the transgression against the commandment, "And you shall not hurt the feelings of one another, but you shall fear your Lord, for I, God, am your Lord."[34] "Can't you take a joke?" falls into the same category: it should never be said. If your husband reacts negatively to your attempt at humor, simply apologize and make it clear that you didn't mean to hurt his feelings. Then be more careful in the future not to joke in that way.

Practical jokes such as hiding someone's watch or tampering with their dinner should always be avoided. Since you know what's going on and the victim doesn't, it is akin to stealing from him[35] and as such may be considered an actual *aveira*. This kind of behavior also erodes trust.

One must be particularly careful not to make hurtful jokes in public ("Naftali doesn't pay tuition for the kids. That's why he remains unemployed—he doesn't want to jeopardize his subsidy!"). The embarrassment one causes in this way can be a very serious transgression.[36] Moreover, it is inevitable that one's husband will feel some level of discomfort as a result of such "humor"—anywhere from a mild sensation of unease to a severe reaction of hostility. Rather than increasing affection in the marriage, this sort of humor destroys closeness. Appropriate, closeness-building humor always evokes a smile or a chuckle. It warms one up and has a healing effect emotionally and even physically. "A merry heart is good healing medicine" we learn from our Sages.[37] This is the only kind of humor a wife should use.

38. Use Positive Imagery

A wife can increase her affection toward her husband by using positive imagery—generating pictures in her own mind which are pleasing and lovable. For example, suppose her husband promised to come home quickly after *shul* on *motzo'ei* Shabbos to help her tidy up for their *melava malka*. Instead of arriving earlier than usual he is detained, leaving her wondering just what is keeping him. Not having the ability to know for sure what is causing the delay, the wife uses her imagination. "He's probably hanging around 'shmoozing' with the men so he can get out of helping me tonight," she thinks to herself. As she thinks these thoughts she gets tense and angry. She can feel herself getting increasingly upset with every passing minute. When he finally arrives, her annoyance is obvious. Having worked herself up with her imagination for the past twenty minutes, she is now hostile and distant from her spouse.

However, this woman had another choice. We all have the ability to control our thoughts and choose their direction.[38] We can decide to aggravate ourselves or to make ourselves relaxed and happy. Thus, this wife might have decided to keep herself calm and caring by thinking that her husband must have been detained by an important mitzvah. She might have pictured him taking some elderly man home or helping a *baal teshuvah* with an important question. While she imagines such scenes, she remains in a pleasant mood. When her husband arrives and offers his explanations for being late, she is receptive and positive. If it turns out that he forgot to come home early and was in fact just "shmoozing" with the men, the wife may be disappointed and irritated. However, having NOT spent the previous twenty minutes working herself into a temper, she will not overreact even if she finds his behavior unacceptable. Moreover, if it turns out that he did have a fully reasonable explanation for the tardiness, she will not have wasted her emotional energy by angering herself unnecessarily. In addition, she will have heeded the advice of our Sages who teach us to judge others favorably.[39]

A general rule is to choose the positive possibility over a negative one whenever there is a doubt. If your husband looks a little depressed and you haven't had a chance to discuss things with him, assume that he is upset about something minor. Don't assume that he is upset with you or that he has a major problem. Always choose the brighter possibility. If your husband says he likes your dress, assume he means what he says. Don't assume that he has an ulterior motive for making the compliment or that he only likes it because he has bad taste. Interpret all words and behaviors in the best possible light. By regularly making such positive evaluations, a wife keeps herself feeling close to her husband.

Positive imagery can also be used to turn negative feelings into loving ones. For example, a wife may find herself holding on to angry feelings after an unpleasant interchange with her husband. She knows that she should not do so, but rather should quickly forget the incident and get on with things. However, she doesn't know how to forget her pain. She keeps picturing the scene over and over, thinking about what he said, what she said, what she should have said and so on. Then she suddenly remembers that positive imagery can help change an emotional state. She decides to concentrate on the memory of her wedding day. She pictures how handsome her husband was, how happy she was, and how close they felt. She concentrates on this picture until she can almost re-experience all of the exciting and happy sensations. Then she notices that—like magic—she is no longer angry at her husband, but is able to feel love for him again.

Example 1

wrong:

> wife (to herself): "That husband of mine has no sechel! He spends money as if it grows on trees. Now he's buying a computer we don't need. All he wants is a toy for himself and the children. He doesn't care what kind of financial mess he gets us into."

right:

> wife: "Oy, that husband of mine! He's always overspending. The latest is this computer–a toy for him and the children. Actually, he's just like a little boy when it comes to such things. I

can just picture him when he was five–impish smile, big brown eyes, curly auburn hair, freckles, and all. His mother must have loved him to bits! He's still kind of cute, I must admit. Well, he's lucky he's lovable or else he'd be in really big trouble with me!"

Example 2

wrong:

> *wife:* "He never offers to help me even if he sees I'm totally overburdened. He's self-centered and selfish and uncaring. He puts no effort into this relationship at all. He acts like he's the king and I'm the slave! I'm sick of it."

right:

> *wife:* "What kind of picture can I generate that will stop me from being furious with my husband? Let me see...why don't I picture him as I'd like him to be...yes, I can see it now: he's running after me to find out what he can do to make me happy. He's bringing me everything I ask for and he's taking over all my unpleasant tasks. What a great husband! He's cleaning up his messy office; he's cleaning the whole house; he's putting the children to bed–this is really pleasant. I feel myself calming down already. It makes me feel good to pretend even if it never happens."

Comment:

The husband in the first example is provoking his wife by his behavior. Certainly this wife is entitled to be furious and frustrated if her husband is constantly overspending. If she has tried for many years to help him overcome this problem and has failed in her attempts, she must now decide how this problem is going to affect her. Is it so intolerable that she cannot go on with the marriage (e.g., his money mismanagement results in lack of appropriate food, clothing, and shelter for the family)? Or is it unpleasant but tolerable? If she decides that she will remain married to him, then she must make another choice. Will she allow this fault in her husband to make her miserable, or will she somehow find a way to be happy and loving despite it?

It is obviously more pleasant to feel happy and loving than to feel miserable but "right." Oddly enough, many people have so much invested in being "right" that they don't care if they are miserable! The "wrong" dialogue depicts a woman like this. She knows that her husband is spending inappropriately, and she is correct in her assessment of him. She is all ready for the usual fight they have when expenditures are made. Even though this fight has failed to resolve the issue for the past ten years, she has not given up using this strategy. The couple is stressed by the repetitive cycle of arguments, and each fight contributes to a lessening of affection in the marriage.

In the "right" dialogue, the woman has decided to choose peace of mind over being "right." She also realizes that her husband is indulging inappropriately and causing the family budget to suffer as usual. However, she has given up trying to change this characteristic since her previous efforts all met with failure. She now accepts that this is the way her husband is. She feels that his good points outweigh his bad ones and still wants to enjoy *shalom bayis* with him. To help herself refrain from experiencing negative and angry emotions, she pictures her husband as he might have been in childhood. She conjures up a lovable image, transfers it to his current state, and experiences a closeness toward him. Her reward is the pleasant feelings that she enjoys as a result of her use of imagery. Affection is strengthened because of this and because she has decided to refrain from the old pattern of fighting unproductively. If she prefers, she can indulge in the angry and self-righteous feelings that are more natural to this sort of occasion, thus remaining more "real" and less "artificial." However, apart from being natural, this route offers no benefits to the woman or to her marriage. Sometimes a little bit of "unnatural" behavior is a more productive alternative.

The second example also presents a case in which the wife is unable to modify her husband's behavior. The "wrong" wife increases her own unhappiness by focusing her mind on the badness of her spouse. The "right" wife experiments with a positive imagery technique to see how it makes her feel. She does, in fact, begin to unwind and relax as she imagines things the way she'd like them to be. This is typical of positive imagery—our imaginations really do affect us strongly, causing our bodies to respond as if the events are really happening. If her husband cannot or will not provide her with certain satisfactions, she can provide herself with what she needs simply by picturing things the way she needs them to be. Even after her pleasant interlude, when she confronts the reality that her husband is not behaving as she desires, her body and mind are still relaxed from the refreshment she has provided with her mental pictures. In this state, her anger evaporates or at least takes a back seat to more tranquil emotions. She can regenerate this picture as often as she likes to provide herself with a happy feeling or escape from an unhappy one.

A wife can use imagery in this way when there is no alternative but to be miserable. Not all behaviors are subject to change. An *aizer k'negdo* can use her techniques to influence her husband toward improved behaviors, but she cannot guarantee success in each area. Her husband will not become a perfect human being as a result of living with her any more than she will become a perfect human being. There is no such creature. Thus, she will have to decide how to live with certain faults that are bound to exist. If she thinks she can't live with any faults in her husband, then she must do without a husband, since there is no man in the world who doesn't have faults (just as there is no woman who doesn't have them!). We are all entitled to be loved despite our imperfections. Positive imagery can help a wife to tolerate the imperfections of her husband and to increase affection for him.

39. Act Interested

When a wife is interested in her husband's activities, she acts as a strong source of encouragement and support for him. His response to this support is to feel affectionate toward her. Her interest simultaneously brings her close to him, since people enjoy being with others who share their priorities and concerns.

Even if she doesn't feel genuine interest at first, but only ACTS as if she is interested, she herself will be influenced by her act. Suppose a wife asks her husband what he has been learning lately. The subject turns out to be too theoretical for her taste, but now her husband is carrying on enthusiastically with his description of it. The wife will nonetheless feel close to him as he speaks to her, his face aglow, his eyes sparkling, his presence animated. Even if she has no interest in the words themselves, it is pleasant to be near a person who is excited. Just as she enjoys the enthusiasm of her youngster when he is learning his *aleph-bais*, even though she finds the repetition of the letters boring in itself, a woman can find her husband's elevated mood endearing as well.

The *aizer k'negdo* can actually help her husband to reach greater heights through demonstrating her interest in his performance. Her interest helps him to maintain his own enthusiasm. "Enthusiasm generates power. A person with enthusiasm is able to overcome laziness and pursue wisdom and higher spiritual levels."[40] Her inquiries concerning his activities, her eye contact, and the time that she gives him while he replies, act as strong forms of positive reinforcement and attention. You know how you feel when someone asks you to tell them about your day (or your project, or your work). You are grateful for the opportunity to talk about something which interests you. You feel warm toward the person who was kind enough to ask you. You feel energized by the chance to put your experiences and impressions into words. Through your discussion you may also gain additional insights or ideas and renewed enthusiasm. These are all the benefits which accrue to your husband when you show interest in his life.

Example 1

wrong:

> *wife: "So, Zev, tell me: how are things?"*

right:

> *wife: "Zev, how did your meeting go with Mr. Blume? Did you arrange anything with him?"*

Example 2

wrong:

> *husband: "...so then we started to explore the ramifications of that statement and the results were just amazing!"*

wife: "Really? By the way, Reuven, did you pick up any milk on the way home?"

right:

husband: "...so then we started to explore the ramifications of that statement and the results were just amazing!"

wife: "Really? It sounds very exciting! You must really enjoy it when you get an opportunity to match minds with brilliant people."

Comment:

There is a skill involved in showing interest. A mother may think she is showing interest in her child's day when she asks, "How was school today?" However, the usual response, "Fine," indicates that the child perceives the question to be a simple ritual. He doesn't feel the keen interest of his parent. On the other hand, if Mommy asks, "What did your teacher say about your book report?" the child knows that Mommy is actively following his scholastic efforts and is interested in what is going on in his life. In order to show interest, a wife must keep track of what her husband is doing and ask him specific questions concerning those activities. These questions should not be of a prying nature, of course, but light inquiries which demonstrate interest (not nosiness!).

Most importantly, a wife must look like she's listening to her husband's reply. Looking him in the eye and giving him a few minutes of her precious time conveys interest. Making an intelligent response to his comments, or asking an appropriate question, also shows involvement. Don't get lost in your own thoughts and forget to acknowledge that your husband was speaking! Even a well-considered "Oh," can suffice.

If your husband actually asks for your attention ("Come look at what I've done to the yard, Minna"), then try to interrupt your own activity for a moment to accommodate his wishes. A housewife can easily be so busy that she tends to say, "Not now" all too frequently. Whenever possible, do make the interruption for the sake of developing affection in your marriage.

In the second example, the "wrong" wife quickly changes the subject her husband is discussing. This abrupt cut-off leaves him feeling that she isn't very interested in what he has to say. The "right" wife reflects back to him what his mood is and what his meaning seems to be. This makes her husband feel well attended. Her few lines of feedback, demonstrating that she understands what he must have felt, makes him feel that she is really on his "wavelength" and that she really cares about what he says. It only takes a sentence or two to convey this message—an easy investment for such a large payoff.

40. Make Yourself Attractive

When a young man is looking for a wife, he generally hopes to find someone "attractive." Most young men consider it important that their future wife be slim and nicely dressed. If she has a becoming hairstyle and a pretty face, all the better. Why do men care what their bride will look like? Why don't they simply concentrate on the really important things like good *middos* and *yiras shomayim*?

It's not that most men are superficial. They know they must look for important qualities in a Jewish wife. They know the business of marriage is serious and requires careful judgment rather than impulsive reactions. Yet they hope that they can find a combination of outstanding personal characteristics and beauty. They want to feel attracted to the woman they will share life with. Obviously this includes the normal physical attraction that pulls men and women together, but it also includes a general dynamic of the relationship. A man may find it more pleasant and therefore easier to be in the presence of a woman he finds attractive. Just as it is easier in some ways to deal with a beautiful child—just gazing upon such a child results in a feeling of affection ("Oh, he's so cute I could just take him home with me!")—it is easier to love an attractive spouse. The Talmud itself acknowledges the importance of an attractive wife, stating: "A beautiful wife makes happiness, and her husband's days are doubled."[41]

Fortunately, it is not that hard to be an attractive person. Most people fall within the average range of beauty—very few are unusually pretty and very few are unusually ugly. Thus, almost all women can make themselves attractive to their husbands by following a few basic rules.

To begin with, a woman can dress in a way which pleases her husband. In fact, the Torah teaches us that a woman should beautify herself for her husband.[42] This means that if your husband finds "model coats" (also called "housecoats") attractive, then by all means wear them frequently. On the other hand, if he prefers to see a woman wearing clothes, then wear wash-and-wear clothes around the house. You may have to ask him. Don't assume that since he has never complained, he's quite happy to come home each day to someone in a housecoat. Perhaps he thinks that he has no choice or that you have to dress that way just for practicality. Be careful to find out what his opinion really is. Particularly if he works in an office environment where he sees women dressed beautifully (and probably provocatively) all day, he may want to come home to someone who is also dressed nicely. Even if he studies in Kollel and never sees another woman, he may prefer that his wife be nicely dressed. He preferred it when he was courting her, so he may still prefer it twenty years later. She was careful to look her best when she was trying to win his love, so she must still be careful twenty years later if she wants to maintain this affection.

Another thing a wife can do to make herself attractive is to wear an attractive *sheitl* or head covering. Again, make sure it is the style that your own husband likes best. Although we must cover our heads, we needn't look like washerwomen! Some women are very careful to be presentable when they leave the house, but relax their standards considerably when they are in it. This is the opposite of Torah guided behavior.[43] A husband will feel closer and more attracted to a wife who covers her hair in a way which he finds attractive.

A third rule, not so simple, is to remain slim. Almost every man prefers a woman who is not overweight. The fact that your husband is used to your extra poundage does not mean that he is actually pleased by it. Although you needn't look at yourself frequently if you don't want to, he has no choice but to see you when he interacts with you. If what he sees is a fat lady, you can be sure that it interferes at some level with his attachment to you. Hopefully, he has grown to love you solidly enough that your weight poses no actual threat to the stability of the marriage. However, it detracts from the level of affection that could be there. If every time he gazed upon you he saw something which made him happy and proud, it would strengthen his affection for you. Similarly, if every time he looks at you he sees something which gives him a negative sensation, then it naturally detracts from his positive feelings. A woman may also be bothered by her husband's excess weight. You can certainly imagine how having an extremely obese husband would detract from your affection for him: you might be repulsed every time you saw him, despite the fact that he had a wonderful personality. This is how many men feel when they look at overweight women. (Of course, there are some men who are actually attracted to heavy women and don't like to have their wives "too skinny"!) Although your husband has gotten used to your shape and appearance slowly over the years, you can still endear yourself to him more strongly by trying to maintain an attractive physical image.

Example

wrong:

> wife: "Let's be practical. I'm middle-aged now, not the teenager I was when my husband met me. I've had, k'nein hora, seven children. I'm in the house all day cooking and cleaning. Sure I've put on weight! After seven children, who wouldn't? Sure I wear a house dress! Should I put on a party dress to clean the toilets? Look, if he doesn't love me now, after twenty-five years of marriage, the best make-up job in the world won't help! I am what I am–he can take me or leave me."

Comment:

This typical attitude is only a wife's excuse for not making an effort for her husband. She's not willing to look her best for him, but she will still make a major effort when she goes to shul on Shabbos or Yom Tov and for every simcha that she attends. Even when she goes shopping she will make sure she looks nice. Certainly, if she visits with her lady friends she will dress up attractively. Why is her husband not considered as important as all of these other people?

Many women want to feel relaxed in their own homes. It takes effort to "put oneself together," and they would rather not expend that effort in the comfort of their homes where they feel secure enough to be themselves. However, this attitude is similar to the one which causes people to speak ever so nicely to acquaintances and strangers and yet insult and attack their own family members. At home, they "relax" and let themselves be "natural." This kind of relaxation is a basic disrespect for one's family.[44] A Jewish woman should ideally treat her husband (and children) with at least as much respect and consideration as she treats other people. This includes making herself presentable for them. It is no harder to put on a pretty dress than to put on a frumpy one. It is not harder to wash the pretty one (thanks to polyester) than the frumpy one. The same goes for the head covering and items of jewelery. A wife consciously should choose to make herself as attractive as she can comfortably be. Her efforts contribute to the process of developing and maintaining affection in her marital relationship.

41. Have Something to Contribute

People don't normally choose boring people to be their friends. When we spend time with someone, we enjoy his or her company if we find it warm and stimulating. However, if the other person has nothing to say, we soon get bored, even if the person smiles and looks pleasant the whole time. This boredom leads us to avoid that person in the future. It breaks down our companionship.

The same dynamics operate within marriage. When a wife has something to contribute in the way of ideas and discussion, her husband will be more attracted to her. Although they may not sit down for hours at a time discussing important philosophical issues, even passing comments can be more and less interesting. If a wife's conversation tends to center around household functions ("Could you please buy some milk today?" and "I sewed your buttons on your shirt"), her husband can still appreciate her and love her. Nonetheless, he may enjoy her presence even more if she has other things to talk about as well: "Tsvi, I just finished reading that article in the Jewish paper. You're right—it deserves a response. I'm going to type something up tonight."

How does a wife make herself a more interesting person? There are actually many ways. Each one makes her not only more interesting to her husband but also more interesting to herself! Her own life becomes enriched as she extends herself into activities other than housework. This is not to denigrate housework! It is certainly an important duty and a great mitzvah that a woman does for her family. However, if it is her only activity in life, then she is apt to become limited in her conversation and outlook. What else can a busy mother do to develop her potentials while she has the responsibility of little ones at home?

Reading is one activity that she may be able to incorporate into her day. Even if she puts aside only ten or fifteen minutes a day for reading, she will be able to finish many books in the course of a few years. If she chooses interesting material, she will have something to mention to her husband. Any new or provocative idea makes for interesting conversation. Torah literature always offers something worth commenting on.

Listening to Torah tapes is another possible way of incorporating some learning into a busy day. While cooking or cleaning, a wife can sometimes listen to a *shiur* on tape or, in many places, on the telephone and radio stations. If the demands of young children make it difficult to tune in to audio programs, one might be able to arrange to go out of the house to attend a weekly *shiur*. Always make it a point to discuss your learning briefly with your spouse. If a wife is able to get out for a brief time each week, she may also be able to take advantage of the self-improvement courses that are available in many communities. A wife can learn bookkeeping or word processing, knitting or painting, the art of natural cooking or calligraphy. Again, it is important for her to talk about her classroom experiences with her husband.

Another way to add an interesting dimension to your life is to become involved in some project. Whether it is raising funds, visiting the sick, or any other kind of community work, it will provide you with a topic of conversation as well as the rewards of a mitzvah. Projects which make a financial contribution to your marriage, such as part-time employment, home-based retail efforts, or any other paid endeavor, also broaden your horizons beyond the kitchen sink. Thus, whether your involvement is on a volunteer or paid basis, any work you do adds dimension to your life.

A woman can certainly make life interesting for herself and her family even when she restricts her activities to homemaking. A creative homemaker can be busy taking her children to various stimulating programs or creating them in her own home (Jewish story hour?). She can polish and improve her parenting skills through attending parenting groups or reading, thus "professionalizing" her career in mothering (as a Torah mother should).[45] She can learn and practice various crafts, such as needlepoint, sewing, and knitting, and/or she can become an expert in culinary studies, the art of preparing nutritious and delicious snacks and meals. In other words, homemaking is what you make it, and there is no limitation to how stimulating a job it can be. The more a woman applies herself to this "career," the more interesting she becomes to her husband.

Example 1

wrong:

> *husband:* "Esther, I saw a notice about a lecture you might be interested in tonight. I'll babysit if you want to go."

> *wife:* "Thanks, Yisroel, but I think I'll stay home. I've got a lot of laundry yet to do."

right:

> *husband:* "Esther, I saw a notice about a lecture you might be interested in tonight. I'll babysit if you want to go."

> *wife:* "Great! I'd love to go! Do you think you could throw some laundry in the machine for me while I'm gone because there's quite a bit left to do tonight? I'm behind schedule as it is. If you manage to get one more load done while I'm out, it'll help a lot."

Example 2

wrong:

> *husband:* "How's your business going, Shaindel?"

> *wife:* "Fine."

right:

> *husband:* "How's your business going, Shaindel?"

wife: "*Pretty good. I sold quite a bit this month. I'd like to find another distributor, though, because I want to get more variety into my line. Also, I probably should do some more advertising.*"

Comment:

In the first example, the "right" wife overcomes her inertia and decides to attend the lecture. The laundry will wait for her even if her husband can't help her out. Sometimes a woman lets herself be controlled by her housework instead of controlling it. The old saying "A woman's work is never done" is technically true since she could work twenty-four hours a day and still find more to do if she wanted to. The only way to accomplish anything other than housework is to put a limit on the amount of housework you are willing to do. Put the limit in terms of hours as well as tasks. Obviously, certain basics like laundry and meal preparation have to be done each day, but many other aspects of home care are optional. It may be nice to have a freshly washed floor each day, for example, but not crucial. A woman has to create priorities and goals for herself if she hopes to be able to get out of that kitchen! She may have to decide that the beds can remain unmade for a bit while she takes the little ones to the park. Perhaps she'll lower her standards of neatness while she writes her magazine article, or she'll hire household help, if she can afford it, in order to relieve her of some responsibilities. A wife can benefit from making an appointment book for herself which allots time to household tasks and puts in other things she'd like to accomplish as well. By following her schedule and the principles of time-management, she will find that her life becomes more interesting. As she becomes better organized, more time seems to appear and more can be accomplished with her life. All of this attracts her husband to her more as he finds that he is married to a rather interesting and accomplished person!

In the second example, the "wrong" wife does not utilize her extra-curricular activity as a source of conversation between herself and her husband. There's no point in making herself an interesting person if she's not going to share this benefit with her spouse! The "right" wife does use her business experiences as a source of stimulating conversation within her marriage. In this way, she has something interesting to contribute, thus making herself a more interesting companion for her husband.

CHAPTER FIVE
Creating Intimacy

Intimacy refers to the depth and uniqueness of a relationship. A relationship may be characterized by respect, trust, and affection, yet still be a superficial relationship. For example, a woman may have friends whom she respects, trusts, and likes, but doesn't "know" in an intimate sense. She doesn't know their innermost thoughts and feelings, personal history, life challenges, or other intimate details. She may have a large number of such friends, but a truly intimate relationship is very rare. It is a unique liaison which a person forms with only one or two or maybe three people at a time. It usually takes quite a while before a person can know another person well enough to form this kind of bond with them. When the bond is formed, it is as though you have created an extension of your-self—your personal boundaries enlarge to include the feelings and concerns of your intimate partners in life. "Love turns one person into two and two into one."[1] A woman can create this intimate connection with her husband and enjoy the complete-ly unique satisfaction of living life with an intimate partner.

Doesn't intimacy occur naturally within a marriage? After all, as husband and wife create a shared history of struggles, accomplishments, crises, and joyous occasions, don't they begin to merge into one unit? Not necessarily. While this shared history is an important part of the intimate connection, it does not suffice to create it. A true understanding of one's husband is also required, something which develops both through the experience of living together and through open communication. The Talmud alludes to this understanding in terms of the husband's relationship to his wife: "There is one key to every door and one to every woman."[2] Similarly, a wife must find the "key" to her husband in order to become one with him.

Why should a couple strive to achieve an intimate relation-ship? Isn't it adequate if they get along nicely, accomplish things within their own spheres, and feel affectionate toward each other? Although this is all good, it can be better! Intimacy is to friendship what enthusiasm is to work. A person can enjoy his or her work and do it willingly enough. However, if one feels enthusiastic about it, then one will really apply oneself to it and obtain real satisfaction from it. While friendship is certainly pleasant and rewarding, intimacy adds a level of satisfaction and joy to the relationship that completely transforms it. "Love is the greatest pleasure open to man."[3]

Fortunately, there are strategies which can facilitate the

development of intimacy within marriage. When these are employed by the wife, she opens the doors to the establishment of love. If her husband responds to her overtures, they will certainly be able to create a close, intimate marriage relationship.

Techniques

42. Share Your Thoughts and Feelings with Your Spouse

One way to develop closeness is to be open with your husband. Talk to him! Tell him about the pleasant events of your day, the challenges and problems you faced, the projects you are working on, and the things you are learning about. You can discuss the ideas you have and the feelings you experience. The more you share, the more you permit your husband to know and appreciate you. This is a prerequisite for establishing intimacy.

Sometimes, however, a husband has trouble listening to his wife. His mind may be on other things, or he has little time for her. A wife can teach a husband how to listen, if necessary. She can ask him specifically for a few minutes of his time. In addition, she can tell him what she would like from him, whether it be more eye contact ("Could you please look at me while I'm telling you this?"), or some verbal feedback ("Tell me you think it's a great idea"), or facial expression ("I'd like it if you look interested when I speak to you"). After a while, he'll know what you want and will hopefully provide it for you spontaneously. Asking for what you want is perfectly O.K. It in no way lessens the value of what you get.

Sharing feelings also includes sharing your reactions to your husband. You should tell him how his words affect you. If he gives you a compliment, thank him for it generously and let him know that he just made your day. If he says something that hurts you, tell him about that too. Let him know with words (not tears or tirades) that you are hurt when he speaks that way. Not communicating your reactions leaves your spouse unsure of where you stand. Sulking or retreating into yourself leaves him deserted emotionally. An honest, open reaction lets him know exactly what you feel.

This principle also applies to airing grievances. If you don't say what is bothering you, your husband will not know what's on your mind. Not making complaints in order not to get into an argument avoids intimacy as well as arguments. The better route is to make complaints in a civil and loving way rather than in a hostile way. If you use careful communication techniques, you can usually avoid arguing, even when discussing sensitive issues (see chap. 2). However, fear of raising these issues results in gaps in your relationship. The more things you can't or won't discuss, the more superficial your relationship will be.

Example 1

wrong:

> husband: "Did you have a good time at the park with the children?"
>
> wife: "Yes. It was relaxing."

right:

> husband: "Did you have a good time at the park with the children?"
>
> wife: "Yes. Several ladies were there, and we were discussing our plans for the summer. I didn't realize so many people are

taking cottages this year! At first I thought maybe we should too, but when they were discussing the prices I realized it's out of the question. Maybe we should invest in a small plastic pool for the backyard. At least the kids will be able to cool off that way!"

Example 2

wrong:

husband: "You look tired."

wife: "I am."

right:

husband: "You look tired."

wife: "Do I? Actually, I am exhausted, now that you mention it. Maybe I should take vitamins or something. Or maybe I should try sleeping at night!"

Comment:

In the "wrong" dialogue of example one, the wife remains private about her experience of the afternoon. Although occasional private periods are totally acceptable within marriage, one should be careful not to create unnecessarily separate existences. If a wife asks her husband how his meeting was and he says, "Fine," and her typical response to his queries are the same, they soon loose touch with each other's lives. Since they operate in different spheres as it is (the wife spending her day in one environment while her husband is in another), neglecting to share their individual experiences results in increasing separation rather than closeness.

This same point is illustrated in the second example where the "wrong" wife makes as brief a statement as possible while the "right" wife shares her feelings in greater depth, even in such a simple conversation as this. Short but frequent sharing of thoughts and feelings keeps a husband and wife in touch with one another and increases their emotional closeness.

43. Accept Your Husband's Feelings

Accepting someone's feelings is a powerful tool for the creation of intimacy. The recipient of this kind of attention feels truly understood and cared for. When you make a statement and someone corrects you, your normal reaction is to try and explain yourself further. If they continue to contradict and correct you, you end up feeling frustrated and misunderstood. For example, examine the following dialogue between a woman and her friend:

woman: "I hate housework."

friend: "No, you don't hate it—you just don't enjoy it so much."

woman: "No. I really hate it. I can't stand doing it."

friend: "Then your attitude is wrong."

woman: "I know it's not great, but what can you do if you just don't like something?"

friend: "I don't know, but you should do something fast before your children copy the same attitude from you. That can cause problems for all of you."

At the end of such a conversation, the woman probably feels worse than when she started. Her friend does not accept her feelings, but, instead, criticizes her position throughout. Now look at this dialogue and see the difference:

woman: "I hate housework."

friend: "*You do?*"

woman: "*Yes. I find it tedious and boring.*"

friend: "*That must make it hard for you to do it every day!*"

woman: "*You aren't kidding! Since it has to be done, several hours each day are very unpleasant in my life.*"

friend: "*That's really hard. It's awful when you have to do something that you don't enjoy doing.*"

woman: "*Maybe I should take a part-time job and hire someone to help me with housework.*"

friend: "*That's an interesting idea.*"

Now the woman has found a good listener in her friend. This friend accepts each statement the woman makes uncritically. She doesn't offer her own advice or perceptions; she simply acknowledges what the woman is trying to express. She clearly indicates that she heard her and understood her. As a result, the woman probably feels like her friend is really "with" her. She appreciates the uninterrupted listening and feels increasingly close to this companion.

The friend avoided several potential listening mistakes. She did not digress into her own feelings, for example, "Really? I love housework! I just turn on some inspiring music and wash and scrub and really get into it." If she had shared her own feelings in that way, she would have cut her companion short. If she waits for a few more sentences, she will have a more appropriate opportunity to share her own feelings if she desires.

Another error she avoided was sharing her own solutions. Most people have solutions in mind for their problems. If a listener prematurely suggests solutions and offers advice, she often runs into a game of "yes—but." "Why don't you try listening to some tapes when you work; you may find the time goes faster."—"Yes, but I don't have a good tape recorder." "Why don't you get the kids to help out more and save yourself some work?"—"Yes, but they're in school all day and I hate to burden them when they get home." "Why don't you hire help?"—"Yes, but it's too expensive." This game is frustrating for both parties. In fact, if a person has an uninterrupted opportunity to work things through by talking about a problem, she usually comes up with her own valid solutions. Unless you are asked directly, "Please tell me what to do!" it's better not to offer advice.

A third common listening mistake is attempting to preach or teach. "Women only hate housework when they are influenced too much by the secular world. If you wouldn't read secular magazines, you wouldn't feel that you have to do something more glamorous than housework. It's a problem that women bring on themselves by trying to imitate the man's role in life." A speech like this will make the woman feel attacked rather than understood. Once she feels defensive, the friend will have much less power to influence her for the good. We do have an obligation to correct our friends when we see them transgressing in behavior or attitudes ("You shall rebuke your fellow man, and you shall not bear sin because of him").[4] For our rebuke to be effective, however, our friend must feel our love and concern for her. If this lady were to listen patiently while her friend explained her thoughts and feelings, the resultant closeness would enable her to be a positive influence. Then she might be able to point out that her companion's dissatisfaction might stem from her leisure reading material.

A wife who wants to accept her husband's feelings needs to develop this skill of helpful listening. She needs to refrain from offering suggestions and criticisms, teaching, and preaching. Rather she should concentrate on listening passively ("Uh-huh," "Yes," "I see") and nodding her head. She can give feedback, which is a statement or question indicating that she heard what he said ("You mean that you're thinking of changing jobs soon?"). She needs to be patient enough to let him speak without offering her own views and interpretations. Only when he asks for her opinion does she offer it, or she can eventually ask him if he'd like to hear her opinion on the subject if he doesn't ask for it himself. This listening strategy is most appropriate when her husband wants to tell her about something that concerns him. It can also be used, in part, when a husband wants to discuss an issue of mutual concern. In this case, however, the wife will present her own ideas and reactions as well as provide feedback for his statements.

Intimate listening must also occur when the husband's concern is a complaint about his wife. It is one thing to listen when he comes home with an aggravation about his work or learning. However, when his aggravation concerns you personally, the tendency to become defensive results in very poor listening skills. Instead, a wife concentrates on defending herself, correcting her husband's perceptions, criticizing his point of view, and making counterattacks. Naturally, all of these techniques destroy intimacy rather than build it.

Actually, a wife needn't be afraid of her husband's rebuke. In the Talmud, Rabbi Yehudah HaNasi tells us that we should welcome criticism enthusiastically because it can help us to become better people: "Which is the path that a person should choose for himself in life? To love constructive criticism, for where there is constructive criticism there is pleasantness, goodness, and blessings."[5] This means that a wife should be willing to hear her husband out without feeling that she needs to justify herself. Instead, she should endeavor to understand and accept his feelings and try to accommodate his wishes. Even if she feels he is exaggerating his complaint, she can focus on the element of truth it does contain and attempt to improve in that area. He will be grateful for the fact that she listened seriously to him and respected his opinion enough to examine her own behavior. Thus, even a well-attended complaint can increase marital intimacy.

Example

wrong:

> husband: "My job is really getting to me. Either something has got to change or I'm going to quit soon."
>
> wife: "Now calm down. That's no attitude to take. I'm sure you can handle the challenge."
>
> husband: "No, this is too much. I get no respect at all from those people, and I can't take it any more."
>
> wife: "You can take it as long as they pay your salary. We have to eat, you know. Where do you plan on getting another job that's in this city and that's so convenient and satisfying?"
>
> husband: "If I can't get one in this city, we'll just have to move. There's only so much that a person can swallow and still maintain some self-respect."
>
> wife: "I'm not moving anywhere. Our life is here. Don't worry, I respect you even if they don't. Anyway, humility is good for the neshamah."

right:

> *husband: "My job is really getting to me. Either something has to change or I'm going to quit soon."*
>
> *wife: "You sound really upset."*
>
> *husband: "I am. How much abuse does a person have to take just to earn a living?"*
>
> *wife: "I know. It must be very hard for you to deal with."*
>
> *husband: "Well, if I don't get some respect soon, they're going to have to do without me."*
>
> *wife: "I know you'd love to get out of there."*
>
> *husband: "I'd move to another city if I had to-that's how bad it is already."*
>
> *wife: "That's pretty bad, alright."*
>
> *husband: "Maybe I should just go and tell them how I feel."*
>
> *wife: "What do you think will happen then?"*

Comment:

Although the husband's words don't differ that much from dialogue to dialogue, his emotional reaction is sure to differ. In the "wrong" example, he has to deal with his problem at work and with a wife at home who does not support him. He almost has to argue with her just to explain his position. He doesn't feel that she understands him or is on his side. Obviously, her own insecurities and concerns prevent her from being there for him.

In the "right" example, the wife provides plenty of feedback indicating she heard what he said. She doesn't indicate whether she agrees with his position or not. Her personal reaction remains unknown. Her job in this kind of conversation is to help her husband work out his own problem. Of course, this problem also affects her, but she won't be effective in negotiating with him while he is in this agitated state. Thus, it is inappropriate for her to express her real concerns at this particular time because he will not be able to react to them in a mature, realistic manner. In other words, when a husband is upset, it is best to help him calm down by listening to him supportively. In fact, it is considered an act of kindness to calm an angry person.[6] Only when he is completely calm should a wife attempt to enter into a logical discussion with him. At that point, this wife could discuss the practical implications of quitting, moving, and so on.

Even when husband and wife come to the point of negotiation, effective listening is most important. If a wife starts off every sentence summarizing what her husband has just said, he will feel that she hears and understands him. She can even go on to disagree with his statements, but it will still be clear to him that she paid attention to what he had to say. People often negotiate by shouting their own position louder and louder—attempting to make themselves heard. Of course, the distance between two such people remains large. One simple reply starting, "I see. You feel that..." can bring the couple very close together even when they disagree!

A wife who shows her husband that she can accept his feelings permits the development of intimacy in her marital relationship. He feels understood and loved by one who can listen to him express himself as he is. He has found a true friend, an intimate partner in life.

44. Share Activities with Your Husband

Most of us have experienced the pleasure of having a best friend. What differentiates a best friend from other friends and acquaintances? The best friend is one with whom we enjoy an intimate relationship based on understanding and committed companionship. That friend is there in good times and bad, as it says in *Mishlei*: "A friend loves at all times, and as a brother he is born for distress."[7] The best friend is one with whom we share both our thoughts and our activities. We DO things with this person as well as discuss things.

In order to make her husband this kind of friend, a wife must also do things with him. It is not sufficient to only talk to each other about your individual private lives. There must also be a shared life. Shared time need not be excessive: constant togetherness can actually be harmful to a relationship. The same wisdom that applies to friendship applies to the marital relationship: "If you want your companion to hate you, keep visiting him constantly, and if you want him to love you, visit him after long intervals."[8] Obviously, husband and wife who live together are already in danger of seeing too much of each other. However, it often happens that these two people see less of each other than of anyone else! Each leads an independent life and barely has time to spend with his or her spouse. It sometimes happens, on the other hand, that a wife insists that her husband spend large amounts of time with her. This is not necessarily beneficial to their union. As always, finding the happy medium is the preferred path.[9]

Assuming that this medium is found, then what kinds of activities should a husband and wife share? We have already mentioned, in passing, the practice of learning together. This will be explored in depth further on. Something of benefit to the entire family is actually spending family time together. Shabbos might lend itself to this sort of activity, but it does require planning. Even Shabbos can be a day of separate activities for husband and wife, as the husband goes off to *shul* and *shiurim* while his wife tends to the children and goes to her ladies' *shiur*. It is possible for even that day to pass with only a meeting over lunch. In winter, the afternoon nap may be the only activity the couple shares! However, with planning, the family can come together for a story time, a learning time (perhaps choosing a theme such as *middos* development or practical halachah), a walk, an outing to the park, or creative play with the younger children. Your imagination is the limit. The idea is that both husband and wife participate TOGETHER as parents. Don't wait until *Chol HaMoed* —do it every week!

An activity which husband and wife can do together, with or without the family, may be some household project such as creating a vegetable garden, wallpapering or any other decorating project, spring cleaning, or organizing a garage sale. A wife must sit down with her husband and plan the activity, then work alongside him in carrying it out. This brings them closer together.

Even some domestic responsibilities can become pleasant shared activities. Doing the dishes together can provide time for discussion while you work. Cleaning up the yard in spring or shoveling snow in winter can provide exercise and companionship. Cooking the Sunday dinner (if you don't feel like Shabbos leftovers), or preparing the food for any regular or special occasion, can be a creative and enjoyable challenge when done together. If your husband is not accustomed to participating in such tasks, invite him to have a pleasant time with you and see how it works out.

Some couples work on a particular *chessed* project together. This may involve fund-raising and distributing, taking in foster children, *mekareving* young people, or helping a needy family in some way. Whatever the project, when it is done as a team (planning and carrying out the work involved), the couple benefits itself as well as the official objects of its kindness.

Shared activities can be purely leisure activities, *chessed* activities, or business activities. They need not occupy large amounts of time, but they MUST be enjoyable. When husband and wife find something they can do and enjoy together, they have a powerful tool for increasing their marital closeness.

Example

wrong:

> *wife:* "Yossi, I have a great idea. Why don't we take the children to the zoo this afternoon?"

> *husband:* "You can go if you like, but I've really got some work I should do."

> *wife:* "Work! Work! Work! You always have work to do! When do you have time to spend with us? Never!"

right:

> *wife:* "Yossi, I have a great idea. Why don't we take the children to the zoo this afternoon?"

> *husband:* "You can go if you like, but I've really got some work I should do."

wife: "You know, I'd love to spend some time doing something with you today. If the zoo is too big a commitment of time, could you suggest a smaller activity that you would be able to squeeze into your schedule? I miss spending time with you lately."

Comment:

If a wife really wants to be close to her husband, she must convey her desire to be loving in a loving way. Anger only pushes a spouse away. A wife may have to be persistent, though, in her attempts to get her husband to share an activity with her. If he consistently absolutely refuses, she might consult her Rav for advice. Most husbands will not consistently refuse, however, when the invitation is extended in a sincerely friendly way. A wife might first choose to invite her husband to share an activity which she knows he really enjoys ("Shloimi, do you want to walk over to the bakery with me to pick out some treat for later today?"). Even though Shloimi doesn't normally enjoy going for a walk, he might be inclined to do so if the road leads to the sweet shop! If necessary, she can even invite him to do some activity which she herself is not all that interested in. Her main desire at first is to be able to spend time with him. Even if this means that she is a bit bored for fifteen minutes ("Sender, do you want some help with sorting your papers this evening?"), at least she will be with him for a short period of time. Even physical closeness can contribute to increasing emotional closeness. Hopefully, a wife will eventually be able to suggest activities which are truly enjoyable for both parties. These have the most potential for increasing intimacy.

45. Plan for Physical Intimacy

"Marital relations relate to the most ultimate bonds that can possibly be established between two people...Together with other personality factors, it constitutes the cement which transforms two strangers into intimate, loving, lifelong companions, committed to each other and to building a Jewish family."[10]

Marital relations are so important to the establishment of marital unity that they are considered obligatory at times when conception is clearly impossible (i.e., during pregnancy and after menopause).[11] Marital relations create and maintain the intimacy required to make two individuals into one flesh spiritually as well as physically.

Thus, no couple can neglect this domain and hope to experience the complete closeness and oneness which is the goal of Jewish marriage. The laws of *Taharas HaMishpachah* (Family Purity) dictate that a wife is available for physical intimacy only during a certain portion of each month. The Torah teaches: "She will be impure for seven days, so that she will be as dear to him as when she entered the wedding canopy."[12] Yet, despite the restricted period of availability, there are those who do not take full advantage of the non-*niddah* period.

Such couples are making a serious mistake. If they allow life demands or self-neglect to draw their attention away from each other, they are giving priority to something other than their marriage. Their marriage, however, is the power source for all of their other activities in life. It is the most important thing in their world. To treat it as if it comes second or third ultimately means that all other aspects of their lives will suffer.

When physical intimacy is avoided for any length of time, there is a significant risk of damage to the quality of the marital relationship. As well as creating a barrier to full intimacy, the individual marriage partners can begin to doubt their basic attractiveness. This sort of insecurity can lead one to look elsewhere for reassurance. The subsequent threat to marital stability is obvious. All normal human beings need to feel lovable and attractive; marriage is the vehicle for providing adults with this feeling. However, the role of physical intimacy in conveying these important messages cannot be underestimated.

Example

wrong:

> wife: "I'm not sure what to do. I'm not completely satisfied with the intimate side of my marriage, but I don't want to upset my husband by complaining. We never talk about physical intimacy–it's almost too personal a subject."

Comment:

Physical intimacy is an aspect of a marital relationship that requires honest and open negotiation between husband and wife. If husband and wife do not share their feelings with each other about this sensitive topic, they may create unnecessary tension within their relationship. Halachically, a wife must not verbally make an explicit invitation to her husband to have relations with her.[13] However, there is no prohibition against discussing one's intimate life with one's spouse. On the contrary, it is an important part of marital communication. If your needs and desires are not being fulfilled, it is essential that you make this known to your husband. Discussion provides the opportunity for your husband to make his wishes known to you as well.

Few women realize that a wife's rejection of her husband's overtures can cause him deep emotional pain. He often takes the rejection personally rather than just accepting that his wife is not interested in physical closeness at that time. His hurt feelings can cause him to withdraw emotionally, reducing marital happiness significantly. Similarly, men do not know how their wives feel unless their wives tell them. Men and women are very different in this domain, and, therefore, there is much room for miscommunication and misunderstanding. Apart from the general differences between men and women, there are further differences in each individual so that a husband and a wife may, in fact, have very different expectations, desires, needs, and preferences regarding their intimate life. Thus, all of these must be negotiated in a framework of care and trust. The principles of discussion, expression of feelings, compromise, and other problem-solving techniques that apply to all other areas of marital negotiation also apply to planning for physical intimacy.

46. Create a Record of Your Marriage

A wife can take active steps to endear herself to her husband and increase her love for him. The angels sent to Avraham from *Hashem* took this kind of trouble to increase Avraham's affection for his wife. They asked him, "Where is your wife?" They knew, of course, that she remained in her tent due to modesty. They were simply reminding Avraham that his wife possessed this fine *middah* in order to endear her to him.[14]

Anything which a wife does to remind herself of her husband's fine qualities builds love and intimacy. Thus, she may keep a diary in which she records the special and pleasant moments she shares with her spouse. She can use this often to refresh her love for him whenever she re-reads it. (This diary should not record conflicts or unpleasant interactions. If a wife writes down these sort of experiences in order to relieve tension occasionally, she should be careful to destroy such papers very shortly after they are written. They serve no constructive purpose other than the tension-release.) Included in the "love diary" might be little notes that they have exchanged, invitations to special occasions and *simchas*, recorded incidents of humorous episodes, records of important experiences such as the birth of their children, the *brisim*, and first haircuts, birthdays, *bar-mitzvos*, etc. Any highlights of her husband's reactions on these occasions could be described. This book may also contain selected photographs.

In fact, a photograph album is another device useful for reminding oneself of the lovableness of one's husband. A wife can take pictures of her spouse and arrange them in an album in chronological order. Whenever she leafs through these pages she will be able to arouse her feelings of love toward her husband. This album should be separate from those that she creates of the family. The husband can also be included in the family albums, of course. However, that collection of pictures usually focuses on the development of the children and how cute and lovable they are as they grow up. Most women don't bother to make a separate album concentrating on their husbands, apart from their wedding albums. The wedding pictures do, of course, serve the purpose of increasing affection as well. Why stop there? Create a marriage album which can be referred to all the years you are together, recording your passage through life together and forging the bond of shared history.

With the help of modern technology, you may have access to other formats for creating a record of your marriage. Audio tape recorders, video cameras, movie cameras, and whatever else serves to record data (your home computer perhaps?) can be used in creative ways to record the highlights of your marital relationship. You can work on this project alone or with the help of your husband. Either way, it is sure to be an effective technique for enhancing your intimate connection.

Example

wrong:

> *wife: "Who's got time for all that? I barely manage to put things in the baby books I buy for each child. The first was filled, but the next have only a few scribbles in each. I don't even take pictures of the children anymore! What's wrong with just growing old together and leaving it at that?"*

Comment:

Some people just seem to have a great marriage "naturally" without making special efforts. These people are probably blessed with many find *middos*, such as patience and kindness, which contribute in an effortless way to creating a harmonious relationship. If your marriage is already as peaceful and fulfilled as you would like it to be, then you needn't do anything different from what you are already doing to keep it that way.

Most of us, however, find that *shalom bayis* comes only with effort on our parts. We work continuously to improve our *middos* and bring them in line with Torah standards. We negotiate with our husbands to find solutions to conflicts and differences. We experiment with strategies we have learned which might enhance our marital happiness.

For those who are still looking for ways to increase marital love and satisfaction, the marital record is an attractive tool. Yes, it takes a little time and work, but it is enjoyable and it yields very positive results. Some women may like to include their children in the task of collecting material for these records. A family project such as this can only increase feelings of happiness and love within the home. When the children witness the obvious respect and affection the parents have for each other (as demonstrated in the family records), they benefit enormously. When husband and wife sit down together to review this material occasionally, their love will only be strengthened and refreshed. Thus, the results of this kind of activity are certainly worth the effort that must be put into it.

47. Make Yourself Indispensable

Although we have stated previously that a husband does not love a wife because of the functions she fulfills (i.e., cleaning the house, shopping, and so on), this does not mean that these functions are irrelevant to their marriage. It only means that if she is not kind to him personally, she will not be able to win his love simply because she fulfills certain tasks within the socioeconomic structure of marriage.

However, assuming that a woman does treat her husband kindly, she must still have a function in his life if he is to love and appreciate her fully. Rabbi Yose's appreciation of his wife was evident in that he never called her "my wife," but called her, instead, "my home."[15] He realized that she was the creator and maintainer of his home environment, controlling its physical aspects as well as its atmosphere. When he came home, he came into the domain of his wife, whose presence turned the physical dwelling into a true Jewish home.

A wife can create this impression for her husband only if she is actually a "presence" in their house. If she is fortunate enough to have maids who clean the house, baby-sitters who watch the children, cooks who prepare the meals, and gardeners to maintain the exterior of the dwelling, then she herself is relieved of many homemaking responsibilities. Obviously, the woman who must do these tasks herself can earn her husband's appreciation and awareness of her importance in his life quite simply. If, Heaven forbid, she is sick for a few days, he will immediately notice that his household falls apart! He becomes aware of how he depends on her. The wife with all the helpers, on the other hand, might be able to take a two-week vacation without the household changing in any way at all. Thus, she must take even greater care to make a place for herself in her home in order to bind her husband to her.

Why is this so? Part of what maintains an intimate bond is the sense of interdependency two people share. If a husband depends on his wife in some way and is aware of this dependency, he feels more attached to her. It is certainly not necessary for a wife to wash the walls herself so that her husband will feel attached to her! However, if her household help frees her from needing to be in the house, she may end up being out of the house a great deal of the time, day and evening. If her absence becomes more obvious than her presence, she risks losing a place of significance in her husband's eyes. Particularly if the marriage is already weak, he may ask himself, "What do I need her for? The house is well maintained without her. The children are looked after. The meals are prepared. She provides me only with aggravation."

If he really needs her, however, he will tolerate her even if she does cause him aggravation. While he is tolerating her, the marriage has a chance of improving. This is similar to the common case of a woman staying with her husband only because she depends on him financially. She doesn't love him because he provides for her, but she needs him. As long as she stays with him, however, there is the possibility that *shalom bayis* may be attained. How can a woman make herself indispensable? If she is responsible for most of the household management and child care, she is already indispensable. If she is relieved of household tasks, then child care itself is a great responsibility that her husband entrusts her with. Rabbi Chiyah, whose wife would go out of her way to make him miserable, nonetheless brought gifts for this woman whenever he could because he was content that "she raises my children and saves me from sin."[16] Obviously, if a woman has household help because she is busy supporting or helping to support the family financially, then this becomes her indispensable contribution. If she is not helping financially or physically in the house, and is not responsible for child care (either she has no children or they are in school all day or otherwise looked after), she can still make herself indispensable by being home to supervise the staff and being a companion to her husband when he arrives. She can undertake to help him specifically in some way (with his business perhaps), or she can concentrate on being a strong source of encouragement to him in his undertakings. Whatever she does, she must somehow take care to create a special function for herself that her husband will depend on. This facilitates the growth of the intimate bond.

Example

wrong:

> *wife: "I'm not the domestic type. I feel I really need to be out in the community. I've arranged for good household help, and the children are in school most of the day. The little ones have an excellent nanny. My husband works all day. I don't love him less just because he isn't home very much. Why should he love me less just because I'm not here that often either? In the evening he often hasn't even got time for dinner before he goes out again. Should I sacrifice my life to make him feel dependent on me when he doesn't sacrifice his in any way?"*

Comment:

When a husband spends his day earning *parnasah* and his evening learning Torah, or still earning *parnasah*, he benefits his wife in *olam ha'zeh* and in *olam ha'bah*. His work and learning thus become things that she depends upon. This is not necessarily true in the converse situation: her work (if done for her own satisfaction rather than out of financial need) does not benefit him directly, and her community activities do not earn him eternal reward. Her function in life as an *aizer k'negdo* is to be of assistance to her husband in all the ways we have described. This does not preclude her working, doing *chessed* for others, or leaving the house, but her departures and other activities must depend on whether she has first fulfilled her primary task in life. A Jewish marriage does not consist of two independent people leading independent lives.[17]

Husband and wife are to merge into a oneness, functioning as one unit with one purpose: to fulfill *Hashem*'s will. Thus, a Jewish woman should not be thinking in terms of her own personal desires, but rather in terms of what *Hashem* wants of her. Her husband is thinking along the same lines as he chooses to support a Jewish family financially and spiritually rather than finding ways to amuse himself with endless leisure activities. When husband and wife are both motivated to live a Torah life, they put themselves on the best path to marital and personal fulfillment.

The wife in this example feels that her husband makes no sacrifices in his life, while she is called upon to give up her interests and activities. In actuality, a Jewish woman can lead an extremely full life, raising children, doing community work, making income, and utilizing all of her skills and talents. In fact, she may have even greater opportunity for personal fulfillment than her husband has, since her day can be less structured than his in many cases. The only sacrifices she needs to make are those she makes to *Hashem* as she directs her will to His, behaving in ways outlined in the Torah. The Torah does urge a mother to take time to influence her children in the ways of *Yiddishkeit*, just as it urges a wife to take time to build a Jewish home for her husband. A woman can certainly do these things and still find lots of room for individual expression. A husband, too, has a primary obligation to teach his children and create a Jewish home. He is obligated to support his family, which may take many hours of his daily life. As a Jew, he works to fulfill this mitzvah of supporting his family, not to increase his status and honor. If he enjoys his work, that is fine. A woman may also enjoy her daily activities. A man learns Torah to fulfill the commandment to do so. If he enjoys this learning, all the better. (There is, after all, a commandment to be happy.) Thus, a husband is not out working and learning just because he likes to do these things. Many husbands do not, in fact, enjoy their work, and many find that learning takes great effort. Nonetheless, they persevere in these activities because they are obligated to do so. Similarly, a woman must persevere in her obligations as a wife. She should not feel that she is more burdened than her husband. Both were created for one purpose: to fulfill the will of *Hashem*.

48. Focus on Your Husband's Positive Traits

When a woman agrees to marry her spouse, she thinks about what a fine person he is. These thoughts help to create a feeling of love and closeness even though she hardly knows her husband yet. Even before they are married, she may be filled with a feeling of love for the young man. As she holds these thoughts in her mind during the first months of marriage, they help to establish the more mature and true love which will develop through actually living together. The more she imagines her *chasan* as a person possessing superior *middos* and attributes, the more she is able to overlook his actual deficiencies. At first, this concentration on the positive sometimes blinds a person to real faults in her chosen mate. However, this protection against reality doesn't last that long. Soon enough a young wife begins to notice that her husband is only a human being. Then the process of learning to love him as he actually is begins.

A mature wife can actually use the technique of focusing on the positive in order to reignite feelings of intimacy toward her husband. Instead of thinking about all the things that annoy her about him, let her concentrate on his wonderful characteristics as if he has no others. Let her imagine that she is the young *kallah* again, choosing this man because of his lovable attributes. Let her focus her total attention on these positive attributes, firmly pushing aside any negative thought which tries to enter her mind.

Is this only a mind game which attempts to make a bad situation good by pretending it doesn't exist? No! Very often a wife feels distant from her husband only because she has allowed herself to concentrate on the negative and has neglected to make a conscious effort to concentrate on the positive. She has played a cruel "mind game" on herself by allowing herself to succumb to despair and anger.

We choose the thoughts we think.[18] If a woman wants to, she can think thoughts that will make her feel close to her husband. If she wants to, she can think thoughts that will create distance. Since it is impossible to think two thoughts simultaneously, the way to refrain from thinking a negative thought is simply to think a positive one in its place.[19] This takes practice at first, but the exercise is worth the trouble. Thinking positively does not mean that a wife gives up working on real problem areas. Rather, it gives her the optimism and loving attitude required to be successful in working toward change.

Example

wrong:

> *wife: "I can't think positive thoughts about my husband right now. It would be completely phony. All I can think about is how selfish and inconsiderate he is. He has really let me down lately. To pretend that he's wonderful would be ridiculous."*

Comment:

The interesting thing is if this wife were, Heaven forbid, to get divorced from this husband, and he were to find a new wife, that new wife would be able to think of him as "wonderful." In other words, this man can still be considered lovable by someone even though his wife is currently very unhappy about his behavior. She could, if she wanted, be the one to consider him lovable even while she is displeased about certain actions of his.

How would she go about focusing on his lovable characteristics? To begin with, she might sit down with pen and paper and write a list of the positive things that he tends to do and the positive qualities that he has demonstrated over the years. Even if this list is brief, she should imagine that it totally describes the entire person. No negative items should be written on that page. She can read and re-read the page several times a day. In addition, she should imagine that someone whom she respects a great deal has commented to her about the fine qualities of her husband. In her mind, she can picture the scene of this person praising her husband's excellent *middos*. Finally, she should recall that her husband was created by *Hashem*. He has a unique *neshamah*. *Hashem* is the Father of her husband. A parent does not accept that others don't approve of his child. Moreover, her focus on the negative constitutes a negative judgment. The wife must recall her obligation to judge favorably, even if only to merit a favorable judgment for herself.[20] If a wife considers ideas like these, she may be able to encourage herself to concentrate on the positive attributes of her husband.

Once a wife is able to focus on the positive, the results will be rapid. Her anger will dissolve; her despair will depart. She will be able to be close to her husband once more. If a wife is not unhappy to begin with and then chooses to concentrate on the positive qualities of her husband, the effects will be even more rapid and dramatic. Thinking about the positive traits of one's spouse causes a wife to feel intimately connected to him. Her warmth and acceptance will affect her husband as well, drawing him closer to her.

49. Create and Review Your Marital Goals

Goals are an essential component of every marriage. Before two people agree to marry, they meet to see if they will be suitable life partners. Part of their task during this meeting is to establish whether or not they have common aspirations in life—common goals. Usually, a *ben* and *bas* Torah have a vague but important mutual goal: to create a Jewish home. However, the details involved in such a project are varied. What kind of Jewish home shall it be? Will it be a home open to guests and community efforts, or will it be more of a family-centered home? Will Torah study dominate, or will it form the solid background of a businessman's dwelling? Will it be isolated from outside influences and culture, or will it be rooted within the environment at large? These general questions lead to even more detailed queries. How much togetherness do husband and wife expect to share? How many household responsibilities do each of them expect to take on? What sort of financial expectations do they have? What are their life style expectations? How do they like a home to be decorated? What sorts of foods do they want to consume? The questions can go on and on.

A couple may decide that they have many goals in common and that they are suitable marriage partners. However, after living together for several years, they find that they seem to have many different priorities. Whereas the wife originally felt very supportive of her husband's heavy schedule, the demands of several young children have changed her values somewhat. Now she would prefer a husband who could be home more often to relieve her of the total burden of child care. Moreover, the nonmaterialistic notions she held before marriage have changed as well. She wants to be able to buy a larger dwelling for her growing family, as well as new clothes and quality food. She is finding that money is more important to her than it used to be. In addition, being at home so much has increased her awareness of her need for stimulation. As a *kallah*, she thought she would be the ideal *balabusta* and mother. Now she finds that she misses adult companionship and feels tied down to her house and children. She wants a diversion.

The husband, too, may alter his goals and value system as he matures and moves through the life cycle. Perhaps he thought that he would make his life in *kollel* or *chinuch*, but decides after many years that he wants to enter the business world. Some men become more involved in their chosen field than they had thought they ever would be, surprising (and perhaps disappointing) their wives with their total dedication and zealous commitment, which overrides even their family life. Others discover that they are no longer as motivated in their work as they used to be, disappointing their wives with their lowered aspirations.

Thus, both husbands and wives can, through their own processes of change, bring "surprises" into the marriage contract. Each partner may be shocked or even angered at discovering these changes in life goals and directions. A frequent review of life goals and priorities removes the shock from these kinds of discoveries. Staying in touch with the feelings of one's spouse helps to make the inevitable process of change and growth less painful and distancing.

A wife might suggest a biannual meeting to discuss life plans. This can be a pleasant occasion over a special dinner or it can be a relaxing half hour on the living room sofa. If biannual meetings are too frequent for your life style, annual meetings can also be useful—perhaps arranged on your wedding anniversary or just before Rosh Hashanah when one is in the process of self-examination.

The purpose of the meeting is not necessarily to establish common goals. This is not always possible. Although major life style priorities need to be similar (e.g., the desire to raise a family with Torah values vs. secular values; the desire to live in Eretz Yisrael vs. outside of Eretz Yisrael), many of the less important priorities can be divergent. If husband and wife do differ dramatically about several major life goals, they should seek counseling to help them negotiate these differences. However, almost all couples differ in the details of goals. There is no such thing as a husband and wife who feel exactly the same about every single issue in life. Thus, a husband may feel that it is important to have Shabbos guests every week while his wife feels that some weeks should be set aside for family time. This kind of difference does not make or break a marriage. There can be marital happiness even when two people disagree over such an issue or over several such issues. It is most important, however, to communicate about the differences of opinion. What can be dangerous for the relationship is leaving expectations unspoken or spoken only with body language—obvious signs of tension or disapproval. When the issue is brought into the open, the couple can agree to disagree, or they can negotiate a compromise.

Agreeing to disagree means essentially that both husband and wife recognize differences in priorities, but neither is about to change priorities. For example, a wife may acknowledge that her husband likes his underwear ironed like his mother used to do it, but she lets him know that she is simply not prepared to take on that task. Ironing underwear is not one of her goals in life. She has other more important things she would rather do. Husband and wife can safely agree to disagree on very minor issues without sacrificing marital love. However, there is a limit to how many minor issues can remain unsettled. A small number is common in every marriage. But if there are too many such divergent minor priorities, the couple begins to feel the strain.

Compromise is the preferred solution to most divergent goals. Compromise demonstrates to your partner that you are willing to take his thoughts and feelings into consideration. This builds trust and love. In the example of the husband who wants Shabbos guests every week and the wife who wants some family time, they might compromise by agreeing to have guests every Shabbos day but to leave Friday nights for the family; or to have guests every Shabbos but make a special time on Sunday for a family outing; or find some other solution which seems to meet both of their needs approximately, rather than exactly. This is called compromise.

Negotiation of any kind is impossible when the couple does not take time to examine goals. It is important, therefore, to make this exploration a conscious part of your relationship.

Example

wrong:

> *husband: "Leah, let's meet tonight to discuss our plans for the summer."*
>
> *wife: "What's to discuss? The kids are going to camp, you'll have your usual routine, and I'm going to do housework. Discussion over."*

right:

> *husband: "Leah, let's meet tonight to discuss our plans for the summer."*
>
> *wife: "Sure. What time?"*

Comment:

Whenever there is an opportunity to discuss goals, take it! Use this chance to bring up other issues related to making goals. For example, this wife could agree to discuss the summer plans with her husband. Although it may only take three minutes to go over them, these few minutes contribute to the general openness required in an intimate relationship. Now that they're sitting down together, they can also review their feelings about the previous summer or the previous winter and evaluate their current plans in the light of these experiences ("You know, I hardly saw the children last summer because they were so busy in camp. Maybe we should take a cottage for a few weeks and spend some family time together this year."—"You know, this winter was very hard on all of us with that extra financial strain. I really feel like I need a vacation. Maybe you and I could spend a few days together relaxing and visiting parks while the children are in camp"). The wife may also take this chance to mention completely different goal issues ("Binyamin, while we're discussing goals, I wanted to speak to you about Chayah's school for next fall. I'm beginning to think that Early Learning Nursery may not be such a good idea...").

The more you share your hopes, plans, and aspirations with your husband, the greater the intimacy you can achieve with him.

50. Learn and Grow Together

A Jew's purpose in life is to develop his spiritual potential by fulfilling *Hashem*'s will. When a person follows the yearnings of his *neshamah*, he chooses a path which brings him true peace and harmony, for all the paths of Torah lead to peace.[21] When husband and wife follow this path together, then their individual peace is augmented by the peace of *shalom bayis*.

A way of increasing marital intimacy is to share Torah with your spouse. Although men and women have different Torah obligations, there are many aspects of Torah which they have in common. All of the *halachos* pertaining to Shabbos and the *Yomim Tovim*, for example, are relevant to both of them, as are all of the *halachos* concerning one's conduct toward others. Many aspects of Torah study are undertaken by both men and women, such as *Chumash*, *Ne'viim*, *Tehillim*, and *Midrash*. There is certainly no shortage of Torah material for a couple to choose to study together.

If a wife sets aside a small amount of time each day or week to learn with her husband, their marriage can benefit in many ways. To begin with, this becomes part of the "quality time" which they share. It brings husband and wife together in a common activity. However, Torah study is no ordinary activity. It is the foundation of their life. When learning together, they reinforce their most important mutual goal: creating a miniature sanctuary. They rededicate themselves to their aspiration of building a "*bayis ne'eman b'Yisrael.*" Moreover, their learning provides a constant check that they are still on the same wavelength with regard to spiritual matters. This is most important in cases where a woman becomes heavily involved in the physical care of her family, finding little or no time to attend *shiurim* or to read. Without the constant stimulation of Torah input, her level of *Yiddishkeit* may suffer, causing damage to her marriage union.

When a wife learns with her husband, she has an opportunity to discuss many important issues about life in general and their life in particular. This kind of dialogue increases intimacy as the partners have an opportunity to explore each other's most important thoughts and feelings. The self-examination which Torah study engenders also creates the opportunity for growth in Torah and *mitzvos*. When marital partners learn together, the chance of even growth and change is greater. This prevents the strain caused when only one partner desires to increase in observance levels. Although a wife obviously does not study Torah as much as her husband, the small amount of Torah she SHARES with him can be sufficient to keep them on the same path. This is similar to the effect of two friends writing letters to each other from distant cities on a biannual basis. With only these two communications, the friends can maintain the sense of intimacy over many miles and many years. However, should they stop writing, it will only be a brief time before their friendship dissolves. So it is with the wife who learns even a little with her husband. Learning can keep the two marital partners in unity throughout their lives. Without it, they lose a valuable link in their intimate bond.

Example

wrong:

> *wife: "There's no point in my learning with my husband. I don't enjoy the material he's interested in, and he has no patience to learn with me. If he has free time, he learns with our boys. Anyway, we all share in the learning at the* Shabbos *table, so I don't think we need more than that."*

Comment:

The learning that this wife has described is the learning of her husband and her children. Although it certainly affects her (she is rewarded by *Hashem* for encouraging this Torah study),[22] it is not the kind of learning we are discussing—learning which fosters marital intimacy. Learning at the Shabbos table does have the potential to bring husband and wife closer, providing that the wife is a full and active participant in the discussion rather than a passive observer and listener. However, this learning, too, may lack the characteristics required for fostering intimacy. Is the discussion mostly an opportunity for the children to show what they've learned at school? Does it center around a few interesting ideas about the *sidrah* of the week? If it touches on issues relevant to the daily lives of the family members, if it includes a thoughtful discussion of the implication for *middos* or *mitzvah* observance, if it is something that the wife can relate to personally, then it may be sufficient. If not, husband and wife should find another time during the week to learn—perhaps only for five minutes—a subject which the wife finds interesting and relevant.

When a wife sits alone with her husband, learning something which is hers as well as his, she reaps the benefits of shared Torah study. If she just listens to him speak words of Torah, the benefits are very different. She is still in her own world; they have not necessarily merged closer together. Just as a woman who attends a *shiur* does not feel more intimate with the rabbi who gives it, a wife does not become closer to her husband just because she is around HIS Torah. The learning we are talking about here is a shared activity designed to increase marital intimacy.

This concludes the section on techniques for increasing marital happiness. If you were to follow all of the techniques described in these past chapters, certainly you would be doing all that a wife can do to foster *shalom bayis*. As an *aizer k'negdo*, you would be creating the kind of environment in which love and *shalom bayis* could flourish, were your husband to take advantage of it. This, of course, is up to him. He, too, must work to perfect himself if true happiness is to develop between you.

It might be helpful to discuss some of the strategies in this book with him and rate yourselves on your performance in various areas. You can also invite him to read the book for himself, reminding him that all the examples can be read with the roles of husband and wife reversed. If he doesn't accept your invitation, however, don't be discouraged! Your own example can do a great deal to pave the way for the growth of true *shalom bayis*.

CHAPTER SIX
Aizer K'negdo

As we have seen, the *aizer k'negdo* has a wide range of communication techniques available with which she can enhance her marriage. The techniques are essentially Torah-based behaviors exemplifying acts of kindness and *chessed*. An *aizer k'negdo* does her best to fulfill these *halachos* "*bein adam l'chavero*" (between people) within the context of her marital relationship, knowing that this gives her the greatest opportunity to create affection between herself and her husband. Since this goal is of paramount importance, she does not wait for her husband to take the initiative in proper behavior, but is willing to "assist" him by means of her example, by teaching him what she can, and being patient. She tries to be the best person that she can be, working to build personal and marital happiness in her daily life.

Obviously, a woman's task is much easier if she is married to a man who knows how to fulfill his marital obligations as described by our Sages. It is not hard to be married to a man who takes care to honor his wife because he understands that "blessing enters the house only because of her."[1] It is pleasant to be married to one who keeps the mitzvah "one should make his wife happy,"[2] one who fulfills the obligation "never to be sad in his wife's presence,"[3] or one who knows how to "love his wife as himself and honor her more than himself."[4] In other words, if she has found a husband who is able to adhere to the teachings of Torah as they apply to marriage, then she will have a most easy and pleasant task in being the *aizer k'negdo* of that union.

However, the woman who finds herself married to a man who has not yet mastered many of these laws has a much greater challenge. She may feel, "Why should I work so hard on my own *middos* when he makes no effort? Why should I be such a wonderful wife when he is such a poor husband?" No one could blame her for feeling overwhelmed at the obligation to be kind to someone who is less than kind to her. Yet she must also ask herself, "What are my options?"

What choice does a woman have when faced with this kind of difficult situation? One possibility is to refrain from making efforts (since he doesn't "deserve" them). In this case, she will have a very unhappy marriage (since neither partner is trying to make it happy) and, consequently, an unhappy life as well. Another possibility is to leave the marriage. This is occasionally a viable alternative, for instance when the husband is very disturbed and destructive. If he is simply a man with faults, however, she will be disappointed to find that her next husband (if she marries again) also possesses many faults, perhaps even more annoying than those she is currently facing! A third possibility is to accept *Hashem*'s decree—for it is no accident that she is living with this particular husband—and to meet her challenge head-on. This would be similar to the decision of a mother to raise her handicapped offspring. Rather than give it away because the task seems formidable, she accepts what *Hashem* has given her and grows through the experience of raising the child. Similarly, a wife can accept the husband that *Hashem* has sent her and grow through the experience of living with him.

This third option, acceptance, does not mean resignation. Resignation is really the first option—not trying to improve the situation, but rather just accepting a miserable life. Acceptance of the challenge, however, means that a wife continues to make efforts to be the best human being that she can be, continues to try and influence her husband both directly (through negotiations) and indirectly (through her role model and the environment she creates), and continues to seek the help of *Hashem* in making her efforts come to fruition.

In fact, an *aizer k'negdo* who faces a challenging marital situation must always remember that *Hashem* is with her in her struggles. Just as David HaMelech never felt deserted, even in his hardest and most oppressed moments,[5] so an *aizer k'negdo* must ever turn to *Hashem* when she feels wounded or deserted by her husband. We learn that *Hashem* answers all "who call upon Him in truth,"[6] and He surely answers the pleas of a wife who cries to Him for the gift of *shalom bayis*. Thus, in addition to the very real efforts that such a wife must make, she must also be sure to seek the assistance of the *Ribbono Shel Olam.*

Fortunately, most wives do not live with terrible husbands. Most simply live with normal men who have many merits along with their human foibles. Thus, the task of the average *aizer k'negdo* is not formidable. Despite her own human weaknesses and natural limitations, she is generally able to function as a positive influence within her marriage. Great is her accomplishment and satisfaction when she enjoys the fruits of her efforts. The patience, strength, and perseverance of the *aizer k'negdo* win her enormous rewards both in this world and in the World-To-Come.

The *aizer k'negdo,* the Jewish wife, knows that her most important life task is creating a happy home environment. Hers is the house that provides inspiration for all that dwell therein. Her model of fine *middos* and loving kindness brings light not only to her family but to the entire world. The Jewish woman is proud to have the responsibility of being an *aizer*—a"help-mate"; her goal is to be able to live up to that honor and that responsibility. For this, she turns to *Hashem*—her source of help. With *Hashem's* help, may we all be *zocheh* to enjoy *shalom bayis* and build strong Jewish marriages.

FOOTNOTES

Chapter One

1. *Bereshis* 1:18
2. ibid., 21:10
3. *Sotah* 12a
4. *BaMidbar Rabbah* 21:10
5. *Sanhedrin* 109b
6. *Bereshis Rabbah* 18:9
7. Rabbi Tzvi Dov Travis, *The Jewish Marriage,* Empire Press, N.Y., 1985, pg. 23
8. *Shabbos* 31a
9. Rabbi Zelig Pliskin, *Gateway to Happiness,* The Jewish Learning Exchange, N.Y., 1983

Chapter Two

1. *Rambam, Hilchos Ishus* 15:20
2. *Pele Yoetz,* cited by Zelig Pliskin, *Love Your Neighbor,* Aish HaTorah Publications, Jerusalem, Israel, 1977, pg. 21-2
3. *VaYikra* 19:18
4. Rabbi Yisroel Miller, *In Search of the Jewish Woman,* Feldheim Publishers, Jerusalem/New York, 1984, pp. 70
5. ibid.
6. *Yevamos* 63a

7. *Berachos* 57b
8. Rabbi Yisroel Miller, op cit., pp. 46-52
9. *Yevamos* 63a
10. Chofetz Chaim: *Kuntres Nefutzos Yisroel,* cited in *Gateway to Happiness,* op cit., pg. 354
11. *Erichin* 16b
12. *Rambam, Hilchos De'os* 6:8
13. *Bava Metzia* 59a and commentary of *Beis HaBechirah*
14. *Mitzvos HaLevavos* 4:5
15. *VaYikra* 19:18
16. Rabbi Chaim Shmulevitz, cited in *Love Your Neighbor,* op.cit., pg. 310
17. *Bereshis* 18:33
18. *VaYikra* 25:17, commentary of Rabbi Samson Raphael Hirsch
19. *Igeres HaRamban*
20. *Bava Metzia* 59a
21. ibid.
22. *Shemos* 23:5
23. *Sanhedrin* 197a
24. *Chofetz Chaim, Laws of Lashon Hara,* Ch. 2, Par. 1
25. ibid., Ch. 3, Par. 3
26. *Megilas Esther* 1:21
27. *Eliyahu Rabbah* Ch. 9
28. *Kesubos* 67b
29. *Chofetz Chaim, Laws of Lashon Hora,* Ch. 8, Par. 1
30. Samson Raphael Hirsch, *From the Wisdom of Mishlei,* Feldheim Publishers, N.Y., 1976, pg. 141
31. *VaYikra* 19:15
32. *Chofetz Chaim,* Prohibition 13
33. *Pesachim* 3a
34. *Shabbos* 33a
35. "Death and life are in the power of the tongue," *Mishlei* 18:21

36. Rabbi Zelig Pliskin, *Gateway to Happiness,* op. cit., pg. 195
37. Eliyahu Kitov, *The Jew and His Home,* Shengold Publishers, Inc., New York, 1963, pg. 48
38. Chofetz Chaim, *Chomas HaDas,* Ch. 6
39. *VaYikra* 19:15
40. *Shabbos* 127b; Rabbenu Yonah, *Shaarei Teshuvah,* 3rd Gate. Par. 218
41. *Bayis Ne'eman,* pg. 69
42. *Shabbos* 88b
43. *Chullin* 89a
44. *Madregas HaAdam: Nekudas HaEmes,* Ch. 9
45. Sven Wahiroos, *Family Communication,* The New American Library, Inc., N.Y., 1974.

Chapter Three

1. *Bereshis* 2:24
2. *Shulchan Aruch, Even HaEzer* 22
3. *Chullin* 94a
4. *Yoma* 4b
5. *Bava Kama* 93a
6. *Megillah* 28a
7. *Mishnah Berurah* 239:9
8. *Shulchan Aruch, Choshen Mishpat* 228:4
9. *Pesachim* 66a
10. *Bava Metzia* 58b
11. *Shabbos* 88b
12. *Bava Metzia* 59a
13. *Shabbos* 118b and *Rashi*
14. *Bava Metzia* 59a and *Meiri*
15. *Shabbos* 105a
16. *Bava Metzia* 59a
17. *Derech Eretz Zuta,* Ch. 3
18. *Shemos* 23:7

19.   *Sanhedrin* 29a

20.   *Berachos* 4a

21.   *Bava Metzia* 49a; *Shaarey Teshuvah*, 3:183

22.   *Shemos Rabbah* 30

23.   *Avos DeRabbi Nasan* 28

24.   *Shabbos* 88b: *Chullin* 89a

25.   *Rosh Hashanah* 17a

26.   *Bava Kama* 92a

27.   *Shulchan Aruch, Orach Chaim* 606:1; *Shulchan Aruch LeMidos* 16:2; *Mishnah Brurah* 606:1

28.   *Rambam, Hilchos De'os* 1:4

Chapter Four

1.   *Rashi, Pirkei Avos* 3:12; *Rambam, Pirkei Avos* 1:15; *Reshis Chochmah, Shaar HaAnvah* 5

2.   *Pirkei Avos* 1:15

3.   Rabbi Zelig Pliskin, *Gateway to Happiness*, op. cit., pg. 137

4.   *Bava Kama* 92b

5.   Rabbi Zelig Pliskin, *Love Your Neighbor*, op cit., pg. 374

6.   *Rambam, Hilchos De'os* 6:3

7.   *Bereshis Rabbah* 89:7

8.   *Likutei Avraham*, pg. 221 cited in *Love Your Neighbor*, op. cit.

9.   *Bereshis Rabbah* 17:12

10.   *Tanna DeBei Eliyahu Rabbah* 26

11.   *Yevamos* 63b

12.   ibid.

13.   *Chovos HaLevavos*

14.   *Beitzah* 32b

15.   *Shemos* 18:12

16.   *Mishlei* 19:11

17.   *Malachi* 2:14

18. Rabbi Tsvi Dov Travis, *The Jewish Marriage*, N.Y., 1985, pg. 98
19. ibid.
20. *Devarim* 26:11
21. *Likutei Eitzos, Simchah*, No. 38
22. *Pirkei Avos* 1:15
23. *Avos DeRabbi Nassan* 13:4
24. *Pirkei Avos* 1:2
25. Harav Mordechai Eliyahu, *The Paths of Purity*, Jerusalem, 1986
26. *Pirkei Avos* 2:4
27. *Yerushalmi Berachos* 9; *Bava Kama* 92
28. *Taanis* 22a
29. *Pirkei Avos* 1:5
30. *Berachos* 62a
31. *Devarim* 12:18
32. *Shabbos* 30b
33. *Pirkei Avos* 1:5
34. *Chovas HaShemirah* on *VaYikra* 25:17
35. *Shulchan Aruch, Choshen Mishpat* 348:1
36. *Erichin* 16b
37. *Mishlei* 17:22
38. *Likutei Eitzos: Machlokes*, No. 16
39. *Toras Kohanim, Kedoshim* 2:4; *Pirkei Avos* 1:6; *Shevuos* 30a
40. *Chochmah U'Mussar*, Vol. 2, pp. 172
41. *Yevamos* 63b
42. *Taanis* 23b
43. *Midrash Tanchuma, VaYishlach* 5
44. *Kesubos* 59b
45. Rabbi Yisroel Miller, *In Search of the Jewish Woman*, op cit.

Chapter Five

1. R. Yitzchak Abarbanel

2.   *Berachos* 45a
3.   *Sifra Kedoshim*
4.   *VaYikra* 19:17
5.   *Tamid 28a*
6.   Rabbi Zelig Pliskin, *Gateway To Happiness*, op. cit., pp. 215
7.   *Mishlei* 17:17
8.   ibid., 25:17
9.   *Rambam, Hilchos De'os* 1:4
10.   Rabbi Avraham Blumenkrantz, *Gefen Porioh*, New York, 1984, pg. 143
11.   ibid., pg. 142
12.   *Niddah* 31b
13.   *Nedarim* 20b
14.   *Bava Metzia* 87a
15.   *Shabbos* 118b
16.   *Yevamos* 63a
17.   *Kesubos* 59b
18.   Rabbi Zelig Pliskin, *Gateway To Happiness*, op cit., pg. 50
19.   *Likutei Eitzos: Machshavos*, No. 11
20.   *Shavuos* 30a; *Shabbos* 127b
21.   *Mishlei* 3:17
22.   *Berachos* 17a

Chapter Six

1.   *Bava Metzia* 59a
2.   *Devarim* 4:5
3.   *Rambam, Hilchos Ishus* 15:19
4.   *Yevamos* 62b
5.   *Tehillim* 23:4
6.   *Tehillim* 145:18

GLOSSARY

aizer: helper
aizer k'negdo: helper opposite him
aveirah/aveiros: transgression(s)
balabusta: homemaker
bas Yisrael: daughter of Israel
ben Yisrael: son of Israel
bashert: marriage partner chosen by God
chessed: loving kindness
chinuch: education
chasan: engaged or newly married man
Chumash: Five Books of Moses
chupah: wedding canopy
Gemara: Talmud
halachah: Jewish law
halachic: pertaining to Jewish law
ha'olam ha'bah: the world-to-come (the afterlife)
Hashem: God
kallah: engaged or newly wed woman
kashrus: Jewish dietary laws
kedushah: sanctity
kollel: yeshiva for married men

kugel: noodle pudding
lashon hora: gossip
melaveh malkah: Saturday night meal
middah: character trait
mitzvah/mitzvos: commandment(s)
neshamah: soul
niddah: woman in a state of menstrual impurity
orchim: guests
parnasah: income
Ribbono Shel Olam: God
shiur/shiurim: Torah class(es)
shomayim: heaven
shul: synagogue
simchah: joyous occasion
Taharas HaMishpachah: laws of family purity
yetzer hara: evil inclination
yichud: laws regarding separation of men and women
yiras shomayim: fear of God